G000242959

SALES
GENIUS #1

20 top sales professionals
share their best kept secrets
and savviest thinking
on sales, selling and
winning more customers

WRITING MATTERS PUBLISHING

Sales Genius #1

First published in September 2018

Writing Matters Publishing (UK)
info@writingmatterspublishing.com
www.writingmatterspublishing.com

ISBN 978-1-912774-17-3 (Pbk/Amazon)

Editor: Andrew Priestley

Contributors: MaryLou Tyler, Michael Clark, Alison Edgar, Tim Han, James White, Jackie Jarvis, Glen Williamson, Ian Dainty, The Mo Bro's - Keval Dattani, Kunal Dattani and Savan Dattani, Susan Marot, Martin Zeman, Tristan Griffiths, Geoff Hetherington, Steven Shove, James Ker-Reid, David Rothwell, Angus Mac Lennan, Robert J. Smith, Steven Thompson and Andrew Priestley

Contents

Welcome to Sales Genius #1

Marylou Tyler

Yes. No.
Win. Lose.
Go. No-Go.
The role of the sales professional is to create outcomes.
Swiftly.
Proof in point: Take a moment to review all the potential deals you are juggling right now.

Next, put a check mark by all your pipeline deals with NO confirmed date set for the next meeting with your buyer. The check marks represent what I call *maybe-land*. The rest, those pipeline deals with confirmed times to meet with your buyer represent your true deal number. The ones that should be on your opportunity forecast.

What's your true deal number now? Pitiful, I know.

That's where this book comes in.

The efforts to get to a Yes, or No, are becoming less and less effective. But I argue we are the reason for this deficit. Time and time again, we waste our selling time performing meaningless activities. We've lost site of the definitive call-to-action – time on the calendar with your buyer to complete the next step in your sales process.

The exercise you did above proves that being great at sales is not about the number of deals you're working, but rather the number of engaged, on-the-calendar, deals you're working.

Another way to put this, according to sales legend Chet Holmes – "...building a sales machine is not about doing 4,000 things; it's about doing the right 12 things 4,000 times each".

The expert advice presented in this book will help you improve and integrate selling skills with systems, methods, mindset and processes for getting more confirmed time-on-your-calendar activities scheduled. The more belly-to-belly interaction you have with buyers, the better you become at mastering the sales conversation. The better you finesse the sales conversation, the more business you will close. Swiftly. Predictably.

Out of *maybe-land*. Onward to a Yes or No.

As my colleague Jay Abraham says, there are only three ways to grow any business:

1. Increase the number of clients (turn more prospects into paying clients)
2. Increase the average transaction (get clients to buy more at each purchase)
3. Increase the frequency that the average client buys from you (get clients to buy from you more often)

Simple math. Keeping these three revenue pillars in mind and confirming dates/times for your next meeting will focus you on precisely what material from this book to immediately absorb, assemble, activate and optimize – to boost revenue, increase profits, improve cycle time (pipeline lag) and enjoy higher yields (conversion rates).

Marylou Tyler

Fortune 1000 revenue growth expert, bestselling author *Predictable Revenue* (2011) and *Predictable Prospecting* (2016 - McGraw-Hill).

Why Creating Buying Environments And A Strong Sales Culture Is The Key To Rapid Growth

Michael Clark

The way businesses approach the sales process can often be the difference between success and failure. A poor sales culture is a recipe for disaster, so it's important to develop a sales process that creates a fluid, pleasant, and purposeful buying environment.

I've been fortunate enough to be involved in several high-growth businesses, and a common theme in all of them has been a strong sales culture. At the heart of every business, two core things accelerate growth:

1. They genuinely have the best interests of their clients at hear
2. They have a structured passion for delivering the ultimate level of service at scale.

When combined, these two core principles create a powerful sales process.

Genuinely having the client's best interests at heart creates buying environments that build trust, and make it easy for prospects to purchase. Delivering the ultimate level of service at scale creates a sales culture that delights customers, delivers results, and accelerates growth. Together, they deliver a sales system that leads to rapid growth.

Let's dive into these two core principles and see how you can apply the strategies to your own business.

Creating Buying Environments

Simply put, a buying environment is the overall buying experience you create for your prospects and clients throughout their online and offline interactions with your company.

Every interaction a prospect has with your business contributes to your buying environment, from the moment someone first hears about you and your company, through to searching for you online.

Factors such as your website, content, physical brochures, events, sales meetings and onboarding sequences all combine to create a buying environment. Every touch point with a prospect is an opportunity to build trust and deliver value.

The biggest brands understand this concept. For example, before it's acquisition by *Microsoft*, many thought that *LinkedIn's* main source of revenue came from premium subscriptions and advertising. However, these two areas make up just 35% of their turnover. Roughly 65% of their revenue comes from recruitment solutions. *LinkedIn* has over 1,000 salespeople in their European offices, and they're constantly expanding.

Despite being the only global social networking platform that has cornered the professional market, they still require teams of salespeople who are lead by some of the top sales managers and leaders from around the world. Many of *LinkedIn's* leaders are ex-*Fortune 100* directors who know how to dominate market share, and what sales strategies to apply when engaging with practically every type of company.

LinkedIn leverages the valuable insights they acquire from a company's network activity to arm their salespeople with seriously impressive stats on how job seekers are engaging with their prospect's and client's brand. Their sales teams create in-depth personalised reports on what *LinkedIn* calls their *Talent Brand Index*. The *Talent Brand Index* is a proprietary data-driven measure of a company's actual employment brand in the market.

Until *LinkedIn* came onto the scene, there was no such thing as the *Talent Brand Index*. However, they were able to leverage the vast amounts of data to create a buying environment that made brands aware of how poorly perceived (in most cases) they were by passive talent.

Armed with this new information, they packaged up clever products that solve the problem and lock clients into recurring contracts. *LinkedIn* is the only global professional networking site, and nobody has come close to replicating it. As a result, *LinkedIn* has created an affinity with their clients that is hard to break.

"That's great Mike, but they're a massive unicorn business. How does that relate to me?", I hear you ask.

Well, if a juggernaut of a company that dominates the professional social media world requires armies of skilled salespeople equipped with the latest insight reports and valuable tools to engage prospects – and a sales process - so do you!

You may not have millions of data reference points like *LinkedIn*, but you can build out a buying journey for your prospects and clients that allows your company to lead them through their decision making cycle. This will allow you to position yourself as the authority and only specialist solution provider in the marketplace.

Doing this well means that you'll be able to provide the highest levels of customer care to your clients, the next step is to ramp that up so you can scale your business.

The 5 Ts of Every Successful Sales Culture

Many businesses actively avoid the sales process. They are often unprepared for sales conversations, and they think that trying to close a deal isn't in the client's best interests. When they do engage in a sales conversation, they feel like they are being pushy and pressuring their client into pulling their wallet out and handing over their credit card.

A successful sales culture views the sales process in the complete opposite way. If your business can provide solutions and solve problems for people, then it's your duty as a business person to do everything you can to educate your clients on which course of action is best. Successful businesses understand this concept, and they view the sales process as a fundamental step in helping their clients get from where they are right now to where they want to be.

Ultimately, companies succeed in the early stages and experience rapid growth because they find a way to focus on core sales and marketing activities. They create sales and marketing assets that empower their team and give them the ability to recreate the same buying experience time and time again. Everything is documented, so the process is consistent throughout every stage of growth.

Just like building a house, certain predictable things need to happen for it to stand the test of time. I call them the *5Ts* of a *Successful Sales Culture*. If you neglect any one of these five elements, it will be like building a house without the foundations - it just won't work.

As you explore each component, make a note of where you're strong or weak and assess what areas you need to work on to improve your sales culture.

1. Thought Leader
2. Talent
3. Team
4. Targets
5. Training

1. Thought Leader

Having a *Thought Leader*, or *Key Person of Influence*, at the helm of your business makes selling your products and services easier. A *Thought Leader* is considered an authority and expert on a certain subject matter.

A *Thought Leader* needs to do the following:

- Create pitches that cut through the noise.
- Unpack their best ideas into published formats to activate dormant prospects.
- Create product ecosystems that shape their thinking.

- Win awards that make their organisation stand out.
- Form partnerships to enable their business to scale.

Focusing on these five vital areas of business is the first step in getting your business into the top echelon of your industry which is where 80% of the revenue resides. This is why at *Dent* we say. "If you're not a *Key Person of Influence,* your full-time job is to become one."

Although having a *Key Person of Influence* at the helm of the business is the first starting point in creating a strong sales culture, it's not enough. There are four other key aspects of every killer sales culture.

2. Talent

Attracting and retaining top talent will be the make or break of your success. There are certain things that you need to get right to make sure you're ready for the talent when it arrives. It's also important to know what to do to keep them.

3. Team

Entrepreneurship is a team sport, and just like every successful sporting team, your team needs to have fundamental philosophies that drive their success. Everything from how different departments work together through to how your sales team maximise efficiencies on a daily basis needs to be designed and documented.

4. Targets

Knowing your numbers in business is the first step to hitting targets. Top sales cultures know their numbers inside out, from activity and results targets to leads they need from the campaigns they run, and the sales appointments they require each week. Knowing these numbers and monitoring them weekly is essential.

5. Training and Development

Salespeople have a certain level of natural skill, but that will only take them so far. The best sales teams are constantly sharpening their swords on the stone of their market because they know that's where the best opportunity for growth comes from. Having clear scripts and training practices that others can follow to create consistency will give your sales team scale.

As you can see, there's more to selling than simply hiring a salesperson and telling them to get to work. If you want to create a sales system that can sustain rapid growth and help you scale, then you need two things: excellent buying environments, and a strong sales culture.

Creating buying environments starts with having your client's best interests at heart. This requires a mindset shift from seeing the sales process as a necessary evil, to viewing it as a fundamental stage in helping your clients succeed. If you put their interests first, you'll create a powerful buying environment.

However, a powerful buying environment isn't enough. You also need a strong sales culture so you can consistently guide your prospects through the funnel and deliver your product or service. Applying the 5Ts will help you build a culture that will enable you to delight customers and deliver results repeatedly while your business grows.

I hope you find these insights helpful and good luck in applying these strategies to your business!

About Michael Clark

Michael Clark is the *Queensland State Leader* of *Dent Global, Australia*, a global training and advisory company that runs business accelerators for the founders of 6-7 figure revenue service firms. *Dent* is best known for its *Key Person of Influence Accelerator*, designed to help founders and rising stars in business become more visible, valuable and connected in their industries.

For the past 15 years, Michael Clark has been entrenched in entrepreneurial businesses across the globe. He has successfully and repeatedly taken six and seven figure companies to seven and eight figure revenues.

After launching *Dent Global* into the UK 12 years ago, Mike then created the world's first certified *LinkedIn* training company where he scaled the business to 25 trainers that delivered organisation-wide training roll outs for multi-billion dollar brands such as *Barclays, Canon* and *American Express*.

His company was then acquired in 2015 by a Silicon Valley start up in a seven figure deal.

Mike has now moved back to Australia with *Dent* to fuel the next level of growth as they expand into over ten cities around the world.

Mike is the author of *Sales Culture*, a book dedicated to empowering business leaders to build client centric buying environments that create fast growth companies.

Facebook: /MichaelClark03
Twitter: @MikeClark03
LinkedIn: in/MikeClark3
Assess your Influence:
https://scorecard.keypersonofinfluence.com/

Cracking The Cold Call

Alison Edgar

Cold calls – let's face it most people don't like them. They can seem pushy and they're often inconvenient. In case you've been living under a rock and don't know what I'm talking about, a cold call is a phone call from a company or business you don't know, who are trying to sell you something.

It's one of the easiest things to get wrong for anyone working in sales but, it's also not that hard to do it well ... if you know how!

I received a really bad sales call and it inspired me to think about how I make cold calls and what I can do to ensure that they are effective.

This chapter is not designed to name and shame the caller, but rather as a story to educate others.

For the purpose of this text, let's name the cold caller Laura. A few weeks ago, I received an inbound call from Laura, somebody I didn't know, and who wanted to sell me her branding and printing services.

Whenever I receive a sales call at *Team Godmother,* I always start a timer to see how long the caller talks before they engage with me. When you make a cold call, you have to start to build rapport with the customer immediately.

Remember, it's not all about you, you're pitching to someone so don't forget that they're there. Laura spent the first four minutes talking about her company and she missed the all-important topic of what benefits her company would bring to me.

I am quite direct when it comes to sales, and instantly realised that Laura was not considering my needs as a customer whatsoever.

As a business owner, I believe in business karma – I really try to give out what I want back.

If I'm cold calling, I want people to be nice to me. If people cold call me I try to be polite and treat the caller as if it were me. On this call, Laura continued to talk about what her company does, so being nice, I said, *'Just send me an email with the information and I'll take a look'.*

Most people will send you the information and either not follow up or do so without purpose. When Laura sent me the information she *still* didn't mention any of the benefits of working with her.

It's probably one of the worst cold calls and follow-ups I've ever had. It was like watching somebody drowning and not throwing them a life ring. I knew she was struggling, so I decided to help.

First, I sent an email thanking her for the information and I asked how her current strategy is working. I suggested she might benefit from some of my sales training that I offer. Then I left this conversation to one of my employees, to follow up later – this was a nice and gentle approach. She phoned again the following week, and my employee answered the call. Laura knew the buying hierarchy – I'm the decision-maker and my employee is the influencer. It's what happened after this that I really want to draw your attention to.

Laura's second phone call was riddled with the same tactics as last time – *sell, sell, sell* and no research! She did not engage with me at all, nor did she ask what I thought, what I wanted, or what stage I am at in my business. It was so obvious that she did not know anything about me or my business, or even that I have two brands.

The number one thing I want you to take from this is to do your research. You need to know exactly who you are talking to and what their needs are.

Cold calling isn't for everyone. It's tough, often brutal! If you're putting your neck on the line you should at least know who you are talking to – it's not 1986! Use *Google* or *LinkedIn* to find out more about your prospective customers.

Although Laura didn't know anything about me or my company, she did inform me of her branding services, after telling me that I was in need of a rebrand. I asked her *'what is it about my website that needs rebranding?'* – she didn't ask about the history of my brands or when I last updated them. Laura replied, *'Well, your brand looks tired and it's very dated.'*

So of course, I asked which brand, as I have two – one of which hasn't been updated for some time, meaning she could have potentially been correct. When Laura said it was *Alison Edgar – The Entrepreneur's Godmother*, I was shocked as I had only just updated the website. I knew for a fact that the website wasn't *tired*, but her comment itself was extremely blunt and almost rude. It is important at this stage of a cold call not to become defensive. Do not fall into the trap of giving your opinion!

Outbound calls can be effective, but only if you do the research first. If Laura did her research, she would've known that I'm a sales trainer, and my website had just been rebranded.

When your research turns up a great prospect (for Laura it might be someone whose website isn't mobile-friendly or hasn't been updated for five years) you have to find the right way to engage with them.

You would never phone a potential client and say, *'Your website is rubbish, it's not mobile-friendly and it doesn't represent your brand.'* You need the person you're calling to come to that conclusion on their own without being pressured. Use open questions to understand their needs and mindset. Then you can find the right angle.

Remember, when cold calling it can take up to 12 touch points to make a sale.

The purpose of Laura's calls should be to make an appointment and explain the benefits face to face, not to sell straight away.

When I'm making a call to learn about a potential client I tell them exactly who I am, what I do, and how I can benefit them and their business. Knowing the name of the person you want to talk to is essential and is more likely to persuade the gatekeeper to let you past.

Let's look at an example of what I would say to someone whilst making a cold call.

'Hi Jenny, I've had a look on *LinkedIn* and I can see that you have quite a large sales team. The purpose of this call is that I have worked with blue chip companies and also a lot of small businesses and I make a really good impact on sales teams when I do work with them. I just wondered how you currently do your training?'

See what I did there? Not only am I giving an introduction about what I do, but I'm also specifically asking Jenny how she currently trains her teams. This helps me ask open questions like: *'How effective is your training?'* and if Jenny turns around and says that she already has a sales trainer, I can then ask, *'On a scale of 1-5 how likely would you be to change sales trainer? Because what I thought was if I came to see you we could have a discussion as there are potentially things that I could do to complement your existing supplier.'*

Asking open questions creates room for clients to indicate if they're interested or not. If they aren't interested, then you can always ask, *'Do you mind if I ask your reasons as to why you do not want to progress any further?'*

There can be a variety of reasons for someone to decline your business; time, money or it just might not be right for them – this does not mean that it is a *'no'* forever and there may be an opportunity for working together in the future. However, it is essential to respect someone's reasoning. No one will want to be bombarded with phone calls if they are not interested.

Most sales are made between the first and 12th touchpoint (and they are typically made after the fifth). So, following up is an essential part of the process.

Here is what I say at the beginning of a follow-up phone call:

'It's Alison Edgar – The Entrepreneur's Godmother and I am practicing what I teach'.

This shows that I really want to work with whoever I am calling and that I really do practice what I teach. Remember, if someone doesn't get back to you, it doesn't always mean they aren't interested, sometimes people are just busy, and they haven't had time to contact you. What you want to do is test intention – are they still interested or are they avoiding you?

If you cannot get hold of someone by phone, you can always send an email. It's less intrusive – they can respond at their convenience. Again, you can use open questioning techniques to see if they are interested in moving forward: *'How likely do you think this is to go ahead on a scale of 1-5?'.*

Cold calling doesn't have to be a negative experience – it can be a great way to connect with new and potential clients.

If you think that someone could benefit from your products or services, don't be scared of contacting them. Just do not contact them without doing your research first – knowledge is power, and people are more likely to buy from someone that they like, know and trust!

About Alison Edgar

Alison Edgar, Managing Director of *Sales Coaching Solutions* and *The Entrepreneur's Godmother,* is one of the UK's Top 10 *Business Advisers* and #1 in *Sales and Marketing.* Alison is regularly featured on *BBC 1 Breakfast, The Sunday Times, The Telegraph, The Guardian* as well as *BBC Radio 4 Moneybox* and has recently appeared on LBC radio.

She has trained thousands of people nationally and internationally. Her client list ranges from start-ups all the way through to multi-national conglomerates and includes *Dragons' Den* and *Apprentice* winners.

A newly published author, her book *Secrets of Successful Sales,* which explains her *Four Pillars of Sales,* has reached #1 on the *Amazon* best-sellers chart.

Alison is an expert at what she does and has received numerous glowing reviews about her sales courses and her bubbly personality. She is professional, observant, and always strives to offer fantastic customer service. A worthy and trusted sales coach, Alison has truly earnt her status in the industry and is the one and only *Entrepreneur's Godmother.*

https://www.linkedin.com/in/alison-edgar/
https://alisonedgar.com
https://www.facebook.com/theentrepreneursgodmother/
?ref=bookmarks

Why Your Heart is the Secret To Closing More Deals

Tim Han

I firmly believe the traditional way of selling and closing deals, is slowly but surely dying. The reason for that is because there's a missing piece from the saying that goes: "It's not about what you say, but instead it's about how you say it."

I think it goes a step beyond that.

It's not about about *what you say* or *how it's said,* but instead it's about *where it's said from.*

This is honestly the single most important factor to influencing people and closing people. Why? Because it's helping them get exactly what they want from the right place.

That's why I want to share with you what I've learned so far from my journey into sales. This includes how I've been able to sell without having to be pushy, manipulative or sleazy. If you pay close attention to the steps I'll mention below, you'll easily be able to adopt this into your own practice too. By the end of this, not only will you be able to close more deals - but your customers will walk away feeling more happier and satisfied than ever before.

I was 17 when I had my first experience in sales (which is a complete 360 turn from my outlook on sales now) by doing telesales at an insurance company.

I vividly remember the first time I read the script we had to follow when doing the calls. It felt so wrong and completely misaligned with who I was and what I believed. Just to give you some idea, our manager told us to emphasize to the prospect that we were calling from a highly established brand - which I cannot reveal - when we weren't!

This was just one of their manipulation tactics that they used on household owners. The worst part was knowing that the outbound leads that these calls were going to, were to the elderly. Can you imagine that? It was really unlikely that they would have known about these tactics ... so the number of closed deals just kept getting higher. I felt really misaligned and quite disgusted by their manipulative tactics, so within just a few short weeks - I just packed up and left.

My next experience with sales was selling women's shoes under luxury brands. And thanks to my previous experience in the insurance company I just told you about, it's no surprise that I really struggled to approach customers and make sales. Because it was all down to the belief around sales that I created from my past experiences.

The good news is, this can be changed.

Fast forward nine years later, I joined a small team who were selling health supplements. The CEO was a 75 year old man, and from him I got to witness first hand a completely different way to sell to clients.

Everyday he would write heart-centric newsletters to his prospective customers - sharing about how he went through the same issues they did, how he solved it, and how he could help them resolve their issues. What I thought was crazy was that after these emails were sent, we would check out morning reports to find $20,000 - $60,000 in sales! And it was all from those emails that were FAR from what you'd think a typical sales email would be!

That was enough for me to shift my perspective of what it means to sell.

I remember asking him how he managed to persuade his clients to buy from him without being pushy, and here's what he told me: "Because it's all about integrity. I see my customers as my friends, so I recommend to them what it is that they really need." This has stuck with me to this very day.

I can honestly say that this advice of treating your customers like your friends, has made such a huge difference in my most recent business, *Success Insider.*

This is where we train high achievers to 10x their personal growth and helping them to unleash their full potential.

In a single webinar, we've yielded up to £25,000 so far. During 3-day live events, we've made £80,000. From personal 1-1 calls, I've managed to close up to £50,000 from a single person. This is all the while feeling 100% congruent with my message, because by the end of it - my clients can walk away happy (which is what it's all about at the end of the day).

If I were to narrow it down to one thing that's made the biggest difference from the insurance company until now - is something I've coined called *Heartfluencing* - it's being able to come from the heart.

This is about influencing with total integrity and alignment with your heart with what you do.

Trust me, you can't convince anyone to trust you with helping them without your integrity.

Think of it this way; in your clients' minds, they're at Point A wanting to get to Point B through a particular solution. They see salespeople like rusty bicycles - they can get to where they want to go, but their journey wouldn't be smooth, comfortable or even fast.

While on the other hand, as a *heart influencer* - you need to show them there's another option to get there. In this case, you're the private jet - elegant, fast and streamline. When you're able to show people that it is possible for them to take this option, it's like a breath of fresh air and relief for them.

Speaking of which, to this day when I jump on stage - I'm just completely honest with people.

Here's an example: when I'm closing from the stage I ask the audience: "How many of you think I'm going to sell you something today?"

As they put their hands up, I then say: "Well, I'm sorry disappoint. But I'm not here and try to sell you something, I'm here to sell you something today." At this point you can imagine that this is when begin to crack up. Why?

Because they can see that I'm completely open and honest - plus it's something that they just don't expect people to say overall.

If I'm jumping on a 1-1 sales call with potential clients, even there I do the same thing by telling them what they should expect a pitch at the end of the call. Of course I'll also let them know that regardless of what happens at the end, I don't want that to distract them from the questions I'll ask during the call - which will provide them with value either way. Since I've set the expectation at the start, they're not surprised when I go in for the sale at the end. If you do this in your own practice, you'll prevent the scenario when both parties are just sitting there awkwardly because of a sudden pitch.

It's all about being a *Heartfluencer* moving forwards - where you choose to serve and influence from your heart instead of your head. Here are four ways you can start implementing this into your practice:

1. State Management

Prior to jumping on the stage or a 1-1 call, I always make sure I connect to the heart by meditating, visualising the positive impact I can make, and really tuning in from a place of love.

How I do the last one, is picturing myself with someone I love - I take note of what kind of energy I give off.

Like I said before, it's not about what you say or how you say it - it's about where it's said from. People can feel it from a mile away when you're tuning in from this space. And I do all of this, just to show them that the *rusty bike* isn't the only option out there. There's a totally different way to get to Point B that's much faster, streamline and comfortable - via a private jet.

2. Relatability

The problem I find with typical sales people, is that they try too hard to come across as a perfect human being. Seriously, I think that sales people look too much like robots sometimes with how they groom themselves! And the thing is, we just simply can't relate to them.

That's why during calls, I'll often drop hints of character flaws and even some stories now and again. Why? Because your friends see this side of you. If you want to build trust in a 30 minute window (or however long your calls are), you need to be willing to show your human side because it makes you relatable.

3. Becoming Conscious of your Internal Self Talk

Normally, when someone's about to jump on a sales call, they often have this running through their minds: "I want to close this person." And I'll be honest, I've done that in the past.

But since becoming aware of this and tuning in to my heart now, I've redirected my energy into asking myself: "How can I most easily help or serve this person?" By changing this internal self-talk, it's made such a huge difference to how I feel on the call - as well as during the transition into the sale.

So if you've ever felt that sudden awkwardness in your energy when you're transitioning into a sale, this will help.

Think of it this way, if you were recommending a restaurant to a friend, you wouldn't recommend a steakhouse to your friend who's vegan, right? That's why you have to do what's right, and sometimes that even means being willing to turn down clients, and even recommending them to a competitor of yours who could help them more than you can. This is the level of integrity and congruence you need to have.

Own it from the heart.

4. Detach from what you want

A big mistake so many salespeople make that breaks rapport with a prospective customer, is assuming you already know about all the problems that they're going through. An easy way to think about it is when you're at dinner with a phone who's texting on their phone the entire time. There's no connection that way.

So on a call, your prospects can feel when you're not listening to them - even if you're the one whose asked the question! That's why whenever I jump on a call with someone, I completely detach from what I want, and focus entirely on what they want. Their needs become my needs, as opposed to me creating their needs so I can fulfill them.

When you do this, trust me when I say that they'll feel understood because you took the time to listen to them. And this is what's going to help them to trust me as their vehicle to get to their desired destination.

These four points are honestly just the tipping point of how being a *heartfluencer* can dramatically increase your bottom line. But they're my biggest secrets on how to sell high ticket products and services without feeling an ounce of sliminess or sleaziness.

So I promise that if you follow these steps and implement them into your practice, you'll feel the difference. So make sure to keep coming from the heart and experience this newfound connection with yourself and the people you serve moving forwards.

About Tim Han

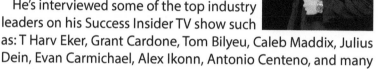

Tim Han is a world-renowned coach, online marketing expert, author, entrepreneur and international speaker.

He is the founder of *Success Insider*, the fastest growing personal development *YouTube* channel across the globe in 2016.

He's interviewed some of the top industry leaders on his Success Insider TV show such as: T Harv Eker, Grant Cardone, Tom Bilyeu, Caleb Maddix, Julius Dein, Evan Carmichael, Alex Ikonn, Antonio Centeno, and many more!

More than 20,000,000 people have watched his videos in the last 18 months and now over 2,000,000 people watch his videos online every month due to his viral growth.

In addition, thousands of his students have gone through his flagship training and courses.

His success has enabled him to speak on stages across the globe, the Houses of Parliament, some of the worlds most prestigious universities, and even meeting the President of Ghana.

Today, *Success Insider* provides the most cutting-edge, results-driven personal development tools, tips and insights – to help high achievers, entrepreneurs.

Youtube: www.successinsider.tv/subscribe
Website: www.successinsider.tv

The 8 Core Sales Disciplines You Need to Develop to Achieve Consistent Sales Success

James White

In my role as a Sales Mentor, I meet lots of businesses monthly. I share ideas and tips on how they can achieve better sales results, but I get asked regularly, how can I achieve sales success consistently James. What is it I need to do to ensure I get results month after month?

Here are the top eight sales disciplines and practices I encourage everyone I work with to adopt and put into practice!

1. You must have a clear sales process

McDonalds have become one of the world's largest brands and companies mainly because of their processes. Processes run and operate so many aspects of what they do. Not only do these processes help staff know exactly what they need to do but they also provide *McDonalds* customers with a comforting feeling and sense of assurance.

Achieving consistent sales success will require you to have a sales process which you use to engage with your prospect and which you can then measure at different stages. Small improvements at each stage of the process will in time equal big improvements in your results. Use a sales process, follow it and measure it and the trappings of success are yours for the taking.

2. You must have some sales disciplines and stick to them

Ask any incredibly successful entrepreneur what the secret to their success is and they will give you several suggestions but hidden amongst most of them will be *disciplines*.

Disciplines are the fuel within successful businesses. Without them, you can have a great product or service, but you won't get to your end destination without the fuel.

I know how hard it is to build these habits and disciplines. The brain is wired to work in the neural pathways it knows. Changing habits and disciplines takes time and you need to train your brain to look at new neural pathways. Gary Keller in his book *The One Thing* indicated that it takes 66 days to create a habit and so moving in a new direction will take some change and effort but trust me its worth it. Create new disciplines which are sales focused and be dedicated in sticking to them and the consistent results will be yours!

3. You need to engage with prospects at the right time

Winning new business is a matter of a persuading a prospect that they can achieve all that they want to with you and your company. It is a combination of several different elements which cause someone to sign an order form.

What is key however to winning any element of business is timing.

There is a wonderful film called *Sliding Doors* which depicts a couple and different aspects occurring in their life because of small episodes of time. It is unlikely that your business will win business consistently on such small episodes of time but timing and doing the right thing at the right time with prospects is essential if you want to achieve consistent sales success.

Too much pressure too soon and you scare people off. Too little too late and they have moved on. Engaging with the right message at the right time is vital if you are to win regularly and you need to develop the skills to know how to do this!

4. You need to have sales plans and be prepared

You can win the odd sale through chance and luck but to win consistently you need to be prepared and have a sales plan. Preparation is essential to engaging with prospects especially if you are busy running your business whilst you are trying to grow it. Without a sales plan, you will meander from enquiry to enquiry picking up some but losing many. Your reputation can also be tarnished by not following up when you say you will or having a clear direction and journey for your prospects to follow.

When you get a new lead what is the plan? How does the lead get responded to and in what timescale? What subtle communications do you send to these prospects to move them through the buying stage and warm them to you and your business.

The savvy business owner even though they are busy takes time to prepare a sales plan and has clear goals at each stage in the journey. Perfect planning prevents poor performance, and this is so true if you want to win consistently.

Prepare well, build a plan and then review the success of it if you want to become a real winner.

5. You need to buy into using clever sales technology

People still buy from people and there will always be a need (certainly within the next five years at least) to get in the car or get on the phone and chat with a prospect.

I am clear that to get consistent sales success you need to develop good sales skills and solid business foundations, but these alone will not allow you to grow and develop whilst you run your business. You must buy in and rely on technology to help you. If you don't then you will get to where you want to, but the journey will take much longer than you ever expect or want. The pace of technology change will continue to evolve at an even faster pace over the coming years as we see growth in robotics, artificial intelligence and automation and so you need to buy into using technology to drive sales and embrace what it can offer you. Technology for technology's sake is not good business sense but gaining insights into the amount of times a prospect has viewed your webpage, downloaded your e-book and clicked on your email over the period of the last few weeks can and will help you win more business.

If you are to succeed, then you need to buy into technology and what it can offer you.

6. You need to sell yourself to achieve sales

I thought for such a long time that sales success wasn't about me but about the company and the service I had. It took me nearly ten years to realise how wrong I was. It was daft of me to think like this when I know that people do business with people, but I've since learned that its vital to sell myself and what I stand for to win new business regularly. I had concerns that I would be seen to be up my own arse or arrogant for talking about what I had done or what I could do but selling yourself is not about arrogance but confidence.

Show casing your knowledge and sharing this freely for others to learn from builds respect for who you are. If this knowledge is built on facts and great wider experience and then outlined in clear speeches, videos, blogs and podcasts with clear value then others will look up to you and want to work with you.

It matters not what your subject area of expertise is, providing what you do is needed by a target market group then selling yourself and becoming an expert in your field will help you win more business on a regular basis.

7. You need to stop making excuses for poor sales results

Whenever I have struggled to achieve success, I have looked for reasons why results didn't happen; and excuses. It was never my fault but an issue with something or someone else. I didn't manage to get the blog written, or the video record-ed because of something else that I had to do. I didn't get a chance to call that potential lead or prospect with the group of people that I met at the recent event because something else stopped me.

I have learnt in recent times there are no excuses for failure.

Making excuses won't turn you from being average to great. Excuses are the bridge between average and achievement and you must decide whether you want to cross the bridge. It's OK to be average and content in what you do but that won't take your business to amazing new heights.

Accepting that it's you who drives your business and its you who can choose where you really want to go is the biggest hurdle.

8. You need to make the time for sales each day

If you find the overall process of selling and sales no longer relevant or just feel it's something you don't have to do, then here is an uncomfortable truth. You are wrong.

Even with technology, social media and the advancements in artificial intelligence, there still exists a need to have sales conversations. The best business people make time for those conversations each week and thrive on the buzz that speaking to someone new gives them. I have learned that speaking to new people and companies is another contact to meet and person to learn about. It enriches my day and broadens my knowledge and horizons and whilst not everyone I speak with is right for me to work with, I know that having these conversations is good for my business.

Making time for sales conversations regularly keeps me grounded and keeps me in touch with my marketplace and what users really think and need. I have learned that to get real success you need to make the time for sales activity.

Whether that is making calls yourself or helping others within your company to interact, you need to make time for it each day. Your monthly targets (I assume you have them) won't appear by magic you have to wave your sales wand and do it daily

So, there are my eight disciplines that you need to develop to achieve consistent sales success! Take these actions whilst at the same time focusing on the problems and wants that your prospects have, and you will be better placed to get the results you want and desire.

About James White

With over 20 years of sales and marketing experience including 14 in running his own businesses, James White knows what it takes achieve business success.

James had a successful career as a Sales and Marketing Director for large international computer networking firms such as *3Com* and delivered results and relationships which gave him a six-figure salary and multi-million-pound budget responsibility before the age of 30.

A major life crisis and the disillusion of corporate life prompted James embark on his own journey as a small business owner in 2005 when he created *InTouch*.

James set out to build and then grow an online, subscription-based software business without major capital investment and without huge sales and marketing resources. He achieved this and built *InTouch* into one of the UK's leading CRM and sales and marketing automation systems and helped over 10,000 businesses in nearly 50 countries worldwide turn their prospects into customers.

James's true passion though has always been to help great companies achieve incredible sales results and in the last 12 months he has set up a new business as a sales mentor and trainer.

James now works with successful small service consultancy businesses who want to improve their sales skills and knowledge to achieve even greater success.

www.jameswhite.business
https://twitter.com/jameswhitesales
https://www.facebook.com/jameswhitesales/
https://www.youtube.com/channel/UCUqzRMkyEC3dLYj5vQtzDEw
https://www.linkedin.com/in/jameswhitesales/

Natural 'Stress Free' Sales Conversations ... With An Attitude And A Structure That Gains Win-Win Outcomes

Jackie Jarvis

"Every big opportunity starts with a small conversation."

In the beginning...

I started my career in sales with small conversations. Small because I, was given a product to sell, no training, some high targets to reach and to be honest I didn't really know what I was doing. In my favour I had always been interested in people and curious about business so asking questions was instinctive.

The product and service I had to sell was something that people and the market were not familiar with at the time, so it was not at all easy to win clients. I had to find a way to make it easier. The pressure was on, sink or swim seemed to be the situation I found myself in.

I didn't want to turn into a pushy sales person. That was not me! I wanted to be myself and I wanted this job to be enjoyable, not pressurised, and stressful. I wondered if I could be myself yet still be successful. Could I be authentic and natural and become the top sales person in the team. This was my challenge to myself.

So, I went ahead and had lots of conversations with people, people that I thought could benefit from what this product and service had to offer. I learnt a lot about what was important to them, the challenges they had and what they most wanted to achieve.

It was from these conversations that I was able to develop a structure that seemed to help people make decisions naturally without any pressure from me. I learnt a way of thinking about selling that helped me to feel relaxed and comfortable. I learnt about the importance of being authentic and true to my own values and ethics. I learnt that I could become the top sales person and later the new sales manager because I was able to both win and keep good clients happy. Others in the team aspired to be able to do what I could do.

I went from having small conversations to creating big opportunities for myself and for my clients. And it was all down to the quality of the conversations I had.

If you think you can't sell you are wrong

Many people think that they can't sell. Whoever you are, you can develop the attitude and use the method that I am about to share with you in any sales situation.

The forgotten art of conversation

Most clients are won after a conversation has taken place between people. It may be a conversation, online, telephone or skype, or face to face. To be good in sales you need to be good at the art of conversation. This may sound easy, but it actually isn't. Having engaging sales conversations may take skill and practice but it actually starts with the right way of thinking about selling and the clients you want to win.

Change the way you think about selling and the way you sell will change

You may hate the idea of selling but love the idea of someone benefiting from the product, service, or skills you have to offer. Becoming aware of the chatter in your head that causes stress is the first step to change.

How do you think about selling? Do you love it or hate it? What thoughts do you have that may be causing stress? Have you ever said this to yourself?

- "I'm not an extrovert, so I can't sell";
- "People hate being sold to";
- "If I try to sell, I might be rejected"; or,
- "Selling is difficult and I don't like it.

To learn to feel relaxed about selling, you must first start thinking about it in a new way. As I said you don't have to be an extrovert or pushy to succeed in sales – you can stay true to your 'authentic' self and still be successful. I am proof of that.

Your thoughts about selling will influence how you feel and how you act, and these thoughts are a result of your own personal experiences, be they good or bad.

Helping not selling – a new way of thinking

Take the focus away from yourself for a second, and just think about how your product or service benefits your clients. It helps people, right?

Selling is all about helping individuals make a decision that is right for them. It is as simple as that. Be curious about how you might be able to help them.

If you enjoy helping people, you can enjoy selling in the same way. Think about it like this, and it transforms negative thoughts into positive ones.

Give Your Sales Conversations Structure

If you listen to natural conversations between people you will see that often there isn't much structure, in fact the opposite. Conversations between people can go all over the place.

Darting from one thing to the next sometimes in a random way. One thing sparks off another. People can talk over each other, often don't listen, can change the subject rapidly, ask random questions, and make comments as they think of them.

Now if your intention is to find out if you could help a new potential client with your product or service you would not necessarily want to lose control over the conversations you have. You would not want them going all over the place and never getting to the point.

Ideally you would want to guide the conversation in a way that would help both parties to gain their desired outcomes.

How can you do this is a natural way?

How can you create a structure but at the same time guide the conversation so effortlessly that it eventually flows into the piece of business and the long-term relationship you want?

Follow the 6-Step Conversation Structure

I am going to explain my 6-step structure – a structure that I developed over 25 years ago to help me to make the most of my sales opportunities. This method helped me to become the top sales person and later the sales manager and trainer in the business. The great thing is this structure still works just as well today as it did back then.

Step 1 - Make a Connection

"Be present with people and you will build better rapport."

People are more likely to buy from somebody they like and trust. The quicker you can make a connection with a person in a sales situation, the more open they will be both towards you, and to what you have to offer.

A connection can be thought of as a feeling of comfort, or rapport. You can influence this connection as you build trust – being natural and authentic are key ingredients.

This feeling of connection needs to be maintained throughout the conversation.

I'm a person not a prospect

It starts with giving your undivided attention and being fully *present*. Being *present* means being fully engaged and focused on the interests and outcomes of the *person* you are with.

Having the intention of wanting to help a person to make the right decision will greatly influence the connection you make without the need for words.

Set up step 2 and 4

A careful set up for step 2 and ultimately step 4, will help you to maintain this connection and ensure that the client is happy to answer your questions. This will help you to guide the conversation and not loose control.

I would like to start by asking you some questions to /explore X and find out what is important to you, then I will explain how Y and Z could help you. Is that OK?

Step 2 – Exploration – Uncover Pain, Need and Desires

"The right questions motivate the desire for change."

This step is all about learning, learning about the person you are meeting, with no judgements or preconceived ideas.

Be open and curious about getting to know who the person is or the people are and what is important to them.

A key element of any successful sales conversation is being able to uncover challenges, frustrations, needs, and desires.

If you do this well, you will help to clarify what is wanted and what is not. This clarity helps to motivate action, be it moving away from pain or towards pleasure.

Once you uncover the gaps between where your potential client is now and where they want to be, they are more likely to be open to your solution.

It is well worth spending time creating the perfect list of questions specifically designed to uncover challenges, needs and priorities.

Once you learn how to ask the right questions, really pay attention to the answers, and clarify exactly what is important, you will not only have someone who really wants to hear what you have to say, but someone who will allow you to give them advice and guidance, ultimately trusting you to help them decide to buy.

Step 3 – Summarise In Your Clients Language

"We all use our own language to make our own meanings."

Be aware of how questions are answered, notice what is emphasised, and the actual words used. Peoples' words and expressions are important to them. Giving a clear summary at the end of the questioning phase will help your prospective client understand what they want. This will show them that you understand fully. People usually love to hear their own words being played back to them.

You may notice nodding as you play back what matters most. When you use a persons' key words, you may notice that they visibly relax, nod, or tell you, 'That's right'.

Taking the time to summarise gives a very strong message of care and understanding. This also helps to maintain that all important connection.

A good summary, along with the gaining of agreement that

you have captured what is important, is probably the most powerful element of this conversation structure.

Is there anything I have missed? Or have I got this right?

This summary can now form the agenda for step 4.

Step 4 – Deliver the Solution Match

"Future clients care about their outcomes, so show how you can help achieve them."

Your proposition, service or product should be a solution to a problem or a need (or both) you have uncovered. Your proposition outlining your solution may take the form of a presentation or dialogue or both. A solution match occurs when a connection or link is made between what is important to your prospective client and what you can fulfil. This is about telling or showing exactly what your solution will do for your prospective client and explaining all the elements in a way that means most to them.

It is about making a fit. The better the fit is communicated, the more chance there is of a positive reaction.

Your proposition description will contain several elements depending on what it is that you are selling. You may also want to include your values and the way you look after your clients.

Step 5 – Gain a Value Agreement

"Make a connection between price and the results that matter."

A primary objective for your sales conversation is to establish the value to your potential clients.

Communicating the price/ fees can be the most difficult part of the whole sales process.

However, if a clear match has been made between what the client wants and needs and what you have to offer presenting the price should be plain sailing. If you clearly articulate and gain agreement on the value, just before the price is presented, it will be seen as an investment not a cost.

Value and price need to balance. If your potential client is confident that they can achieve the promised results, it will be an investment they are willing to make.

Step 6 – Close Naturally

"Closing is comfortable when you approach it naturally step by step."

A sale is not fully 'closed' until your new client has agreed to pay for your product or services.

To close naturally you need to go about it in a series of simple steps. The more you encourage a comfortable *'yes'* as you go through the 6 - step process, the easier it will be to close when you reach the point at which they are ready to go ahead.

For some closing a sale might take a while, it very much depends on your sales cycle, but if you maintain the connection and do your follow up in a timely respectful way, you will give yourself the very best opportunity to be successful. From my experience people value being followed up. (if it is done in the right way, with the right intention, it will not be perceived as chasing).

Finally ...

This 6-step sales conversation structure, when delivered with an attitude of care, and curiosity will yield great returns. Like anything of real value, it takes development work and practice.

I have taught this approach to many business owners, professionals and entrepreneurs who are all ultimately responsible for winning new clients. Many previously thought that they couldn't sell, but, by changing their way of thinking and putting this process into practice, proved to themselves, that they absolutely can!

They all found their small conversations turning into big opportunities.

Natural 'Stress-Free' Selling is a way of selling that allows you to be your authentic self and to relax and enjoy the process.

It is a way of making sure that both you and the people you engage with gain what is most important, a good relationship and results that matter.

About Jackie Jarvis

Jackie Jarvis is a business and client growth coach and runs Mastermind Groups. She primarily helps over loaded SME business owners and their teams take regular time out from working in their business, to regain clarity and focus.

She helps create positive momentum by providing the reflection and accountability framework necessary to ensure desired plans and ambitions are fulfilled, as well as, personal wellbeing maintained.

Client Growth and *Natural Selling* is one of Jackie's specialist areas. She gives talks on *'Natural Stress-Free' Selling* and has created an online course to share this unique methodology.

https://naturalstressfreeselling.com

She is the published author of four books, *85 Inspiring Ways to Market Your Business (2010); Quick Wins in Sales and Marketing (2015); In Pursuit of Slow (2017);* contributor in Best Seller *My Camino Walk #1 (2018)* and the creator of *The Client Growth Club* an online membership site for coaches and consultants. (2018)

Jackie lives in the historic Oxfordshire market town Wallingford, UK, and in her spare time you may find her walking or running along the Thames Path and The Ridgeway.

https://www.linkedin.com/in/jackie-jarvis-b8727212
www.jackiejarvis.co.uk
Twitter @jackiejarvis1

So, What's at Stake?
(It's All in the Mindset)

Glen Williamson

On a recent trip to Europe I found myself training an audience of 36 software sales people.

"Raise your hand if you didn't hit your target last year?" I asked.

Over twenty hands were raised.

"Now, raise your hand if over the last three years you have failed at least once to hit your annual target."

Over 30 hands were raised.

I then proceeded to select a few delegates at random. "Tell me in one sentence, why didn't you hit your target?"

One person replied, "Too many operational problems."

Another lamented, "Our customers lost confidence in the service."

A third piped up, "Not enough support internally!"

And so it went on, excuse after excuse:

- "I had to get involved in too many customer service issues."
- "My targets weren't really realistic."
- "I lack confidence."
- "We can't compete on price."
- "We have to do too much admin."
- "Our product/service is a commodity."
- "Marketing didn't generate nearly enough leads!"

"If halfway through the year where you didn't hit your target, I had put £5M in cash right in front of you and told you that in order to keep the money, all you would have to do is to hit your targets, would you have hit them?" I asked.

Without exception they all agreed that with such an incentive they would have hit their targets. Despite the excuses and explanations, they admitted that they would have found a way through.

It is always the way.

Every time I ask this question I get the same response. But what does this tell us? It tells us that hitting sales targets (or any target) is not necessarily based on the level of skill or opportunity the individual has, but on what is at stake, and what is at stake is a function of your individual mindset.

I shared with the delegates that over the course of a 32 year career in sales I can state, with considerable confidence, that the sales people who consistently deliver sales at acceptable margins for their companies are not the most highly skilled, slick or experienced. They do not necessarily possess the gift of the gab, nor are they pushy or competitive, and they were certainly not *born* to be salesmen.

The ones that can hit and exceed their targets have developed a balance between three essential foundational elements, *Mindset, Skill* and *Fearlessness.* If one of the three is missing, the other two must compensate. If two are missing, then the third had better be awesome. Skill will only get you so far, in fact unless the sale is *complex* you don't need a great deal of skill if the other two elements in this model are fully present.

Ironically, having worked with, trained and coached thousands of sales people across the globe, I find the highest producing sales people seldom have an above average level of expertise in how to sell. If you look at their results, you could be forgiven for expecting a higher level of sales expertise, but typically it is not there. They have simply balanced the three elements well.

My sense as I stood before the delegates was that many of them, if they were given the chance, would have got out of sales without much persuasion. Sales was not a good fit for many of them, but they were offered the opportunity and saw the potential to increase their earnings and have some freedom and they took it. They then adopted a way of being that they believed was consistent with being a sales person. Mostly under-trained in how to sell, they fell into their roles because they were personable, or they had contacts in the industry that might benefit the company. And now in training courses across the world, they sit before me labouring under unrealistic expectations that they have what it takes to deliver good quality revenue for their business and perform at a high level for what is arguably the single most important function in a business: sales.

The result?

A sales team ill equipped to deliver, who operate below expectations and are forced to create a plethora of excuses and justifications to protect themselves. They have never been taught how to communicate and are not fully present in the sales training or in any areas of their lives. In truth there is not much point in training them, because they lack a critical foundational piece that every sales winner has, and that is the right mindset.

At the end of the two-day training I estimate that only twenty percent were competent sales people with the potential to be extraordinary, the perspicacity to take the profession seriously and who possessed the capability to make an impact in their business. The rest were ordinary.

So what needs to change?

Mindset

On one of my recent training courses a sales person shared with me that when he drops in on an existing customer, he feels as though he is imposing on that person's time and shouldn't really be there. So, when he calls on his customer to discuss an opportunity, his empowering context is therefore; I shouldn't be here!

Last week one of my colleagues invited me, last-minute, to join a sales call with a large prospect. We agreed on the objectives of the meeting; who will lead and what we would expect in terms of an outcome.

Then to my surprise, just before the meeting started, she said, "We probably won't win it anyway because they have a close relationship with one of our competitors!"

Her empowering context in a meeting with a major prospect was: we have no chance of winning.

This doesn't work!

Our Mindsets drive our actions, and our actions drive our results. Simply put: weak mindset, weak actions, weak results. Powerful mindset, powerful actions, powerful results.

If you want to know what is stopping your sales people, this cannot be over-emphasised. If you are wondering why they lack motivation, gravitate towards the easy fix, stay in their comfort zones and keep doing the same old same old, the answer is in their mindset. Getting the right mindset into your sales team will go straight to your bottom line.

There is no point in training someone who believes he/she shouldn't be there. They are hardly going to break through, ask powerful questions, make bold requests or have edgy, disruptive conversations, are they?

What is the point of training someone who decides they have no chance of winning before they've even spoken to a customer? It will be apparent in every move they make; every action they take.

So, first we must deal with the mindset.

This culture would have us believe that what we do is all important. We have it that what we do results in what we have, and therefore what and who we become. This flawed view of the world could be described as *Do – Have – Be*.

This needs to be turned on its head and we need to realise that who a person is being in the world generates their actions, rather than their actions generating who they are being, and in turn the actions generate their results. In effect we change the misconceived *Do – Have – Be* to *Be – Do – Have*.

Our mindset evolves through a dance between our values and beliefs. A complex concoction of past experiences, present perceptions and the future we believe we have created for ourselves, which interact moment by moment to create our *empowering context*.

Our empowering context is a significant part of the framework within which we understand the world and our capability to operate within it. A sales professional who is highly skilled will fail to deliver consistent results if his empowering context is *I stand no chance of winning* or *I shouldn't be imposing on this person's time* because he will not, by his very nature, make that additional call, challenge that customers point of view, ask that difficult question or demonstrate courage in the face of 'no'.

If you train a loser, the best you can hope for is a skilful loser.

Contrast this with a sales person with a powerful, positive mindset. They have a different belief which feeds the need to make a difference. They know who they are, why they behave the way they do and are not driven by their egos.

What is impressive about these winners is they are infinitely coachable and trainable, because they know that there is always space to grow. They go above and beyond the call of duty, not because they are asked, but because it is within them to do so. I spent some time with two of them at the training session.

"Yes, I always make sure I provide the customer with clear provable value", said one.

Another said, "I want the best for my customers, even if my solution is not the best, I will guide them toward doing what is best for them."

These sales people were leading the field. They were a pleasure to train, they were open to new ideas, challenged intelligently, gave me some great ideas and were courageous enough to put new ideas into practice, giving me feedback on how effective they were in the weeks following the training.

They are heightened listeners, understanding fully that the heart of a successful sale is not to focus inwardly, but outwardly. Outwardly-focused people get into their buyers' worlds and help their customers to create possibilities. Inwardly focused people are stuck in their own worlds and only allow their customers to see what is possible from the sales person's perspective.

When we are at our best, we are caring, giving, confident and communicative.

We take responsibility.

When we are not at our best, we lack generosity, motivation, drive and imagination. We make excuses.

Our empowering context springs from our mindset, our mindset governs our actions and our actions give us our results.

Sales is unique. We often expect under-prepared people to have persuasive conversations with relative strangers and convince those strangers to part with their money because they value the money they are parting with less than the thing they are getting in return.

To do this successfully, sales people need to operate with a high level of maturity and self-awareness about who they are being in the world, so that they can present themselves with humanity, integrity and authenticity. In doing so, we give the buyer permission to share themselves in the same way, so that we can get to the heart of their challenges.

Sales people must have something at stake. Something that drives them forward and propels them into the right mindset - one which involves a gritty dedication to hard graft, a love of learning and a rock-solid resilience to achieving great accomplishments - so that they will take the right actions at the right time for the right reasons.

And it is all in the mindset.

Webography

Dweck. C. 'What Is Mindset'. Mindset. The New Psychology of Success. New York. Random House. 2006. https://mindsetonline.com/whatis-it/about/ (Accessed 03/08/2018)

Be-Do-Have. Landmark Education.

About Glen Williamson

As a Consultant Sales Director, Sales Trainer and Accredited Master Coach, Glen Williamson currently leads, drives and inspires hundreds of sales professionals and business owners to reach new heights of sales performance.

Taking his 32 years of experience in sales and business development, Glen develops methodologies and strategies that help SME's and sales professionals to exceed their targets while transforming who they are being so that they can live happier, full and more fulfilled

Author of the upcoming book, *With You (Balancing the three elements required to create unstoppable sales professionals)*, Glen is on a mission to make selling the worlds most respected profession.

www.glenwilliamson.co.uk
linkedin.com/in/glenwilliamson1

The GAIM Plan – How To Qualify B2B Executives In Four Easy Steps

Ian Dainty

Introduction

(Clarification – I use the words, *he, him* and *his* as opposed to *him/her* etc., for expediency only. I realize that about 50% of B2B sales people are women, and thankfully so.)

The GAIM Plan came about as I watched so many B2B sales people and managers struggle with different ways about how to talk to senior executives.

If you're like most B2B sales people, you struggle with how to sell your products, once you get in front of your prospect, especially in front of CXO's. There are many different techniques for talking to people, how to qualify a call, how to close, etc.

One of the most famous ones is BANT, which stands for *Budget, Authority, Need* and *Timeframe*. Now, you may need to know all this information, but not until you have qualified your buyer first. I find BANT too salesy, and very difficult to incorporate into a qualifying sales call.

The only way, to really close, is to let the buyer decide. Sales people don't really sell – buyers buy.

In any sales situation however, you can lead the buyer to buy from you, versus your competitor. That is what the *GAIM Plan* will allow you to do.

The GAIM Plan will differentiate you from all of your competitors

The *GAIM Plan* will give you the process you need to execute a flawless interview with a senior executive.

The *GAIM Plan's* real goal is to teach you how to qualify your prospects, so you don't spend a lot of time chasing someone who has no desire to buy.

If you really want to succeed in sales, you need to find a way to qualify people very early in your sales cycle.

The real key in moving any sales situation forward is qualifying. Closing the sale becomes second nature, when you qualify properly. You don't need cheesy closing techniques when you qualify well. Why? Because the prospect will close himself.

The most important thing you need to know, and understand in sales, is this – Get to NO before you get to YES.

Why do you want to get to NO first and fast?

You want to eliminate people that are going to waste your time, and are not going to buy from you, either because they are just tire kicking, or you do not have the product or service they need. As a B2B sales person you want to work only with prospects you believe you can help, and you can build a good business relationship with.

You do, however, want to keep nurturing prospects who you believe will probably buy in the future, but just aren't candidates right now for your products/services. These prospects should be turned over to marketing to keep nurturing

A Powerful Example of *The GAIM Plan*: One of my clients, a long time B2B salesman, used *The GAIM Plan*, and some of the ideas from one of my programs, to close a deal. The CEO did not want his product initially. After taking my program, he went back to the CEO, and this time used *The GAIM Plan* to talk to her. As he walked her through *The GAIM Plan*, he got the order from his client, which was four times his total annual quota.

It does work, and it is powerful.

Let's examine *The GAIM Plan* and see how it can make you and your company become a winner.

The GAIM Plan

The GAIM Plan is an acronym for:

G-oals
A-fflictions
I-mpact
M-eaning

It is important to understand each of these very important words and the impact and meaning they will have on your own sales performance.

Goals

The first thing you should be asking people, in any B2B sales situation, is what their goals are. Now you don't have to ask it in those exact words. There are easier ways to ask this question. As an example, you can ask; "What is it you want to achieve this year?"

However, sometimes, just asking what their goals are will give some astonishing insight into their business ideas and plans.

The idea behind *The GAIM Plan* is to get your prospect/client talking and telling you what he wants to do, and what is holding him back. Many people feel that just asking about his problems and issues is the way to start.

Of course, getting to the issues – or Afflictions – is very important and mandatory. But business people usually don't have afflictions if they don't have goals.

Importantly, people like talking about their goals. So, by understanding what a person's goals or aspirations are, you get a better perspective of that person, his company, and whether there will be a fit for your products/services or not.

You should try and get his top three goals, and what issues he has run across, when trying to achieve each goal.

You could ask, "Why are you doing this now?" If you know the marketplace you are in, and generally why people buy your products and services, you probably already know the answer.

But this will give you an insight into why this particular prospect wants to buy or not.

Remember, in any sales call, or in fact in any communication, learn to understand before being understood. Therefore, it is mandatory for you to get into the reasons why someone is buying.

You will find, by asking simple questions like these, that your prospect will want to share his goals and even his dreams with you. You can't be shy about asking these questions.

Once you have unearthed his goals, then you move on to the afflictions that may be stopping him from attaining his goals.

Afflictions

An *affliction* is a word that covers all of the terms like, issues, problems, roadblocks, concerns, etc. that your prospect is facing, in trying to reach his goals. What you need to do is uncover the afflictions that your prospect is encountering, or will face, as he moves toward each goal.

The simplest way to uncover these afflictions is simply ask your prospect. Ask him, "What issues or obstacles do you see that you need to overcome in order for you to reach your goals?"

You will probably get a myriad of issues. Sometimes, your prospect won't even know what the issues are. Here is where you can help him to discover some of these roadblocks. You have to lead him down that path.

Because you know your products/services well, and the issues that your other clients faced before they bought your products/services, you can help lead your prospect down the right path. However, most of the time he will know what the afflictions are, and will elaborate them to you.

It is imperative that you unearth as many issues as you can here. Remember, you are qualifying the prospect here, to ensure that he is a fit for your products/services.

Then you must prioritize his goals and issues. Only work on his top three goals, as you will get too bogged down if you try and work on any more. And you must ask him what his top three goals are, do not make any assumptions here.

Once you believe you have uncovered his goals and afflictions, and what order of importance they are to your prospect, then you move onto finding the impact these issues will have on his goals.

Impact

This area can touch on some very sensitive issues for the prospect, and most sales people omit it when they are qualifying a prospect. But if you omit this factor, then you are going to find that you will end up wasting a lot of your time chasing prospects, who are not going to buy from you.

Here is a good example of a sales rep who didn't ask this question.

A B2B sales rep sold software for tracking trucks, ensuring they went to the right destinations. As the sales rep was questioning the prospect, who owned a bunch of *Dollar Stores,* the owner acknowledged that many times his trucks didn't end up at the right store.

So instead of asking the impact this had on the prospect's business, the sales rep thanked the business owner, and hustled back to his office to write a lengthy proposal about how his company's software could solve this problem for him.

Once the business owner received the proposal, he contacted the sales rep, to tell him that he didn't need his software. The sales rep was totally perplexed, and of course asked why not.

The owner told him that although the trucks went to the wrong stores numerous times, it had no impact on his business. Why, because the store managers simply emptied the trucks and sold the merchandise anyway.

You have to ask what the impact will be, if that particular problem is not resolved. And you need to ask this about all of the issues your prospect brings up.

There are two questions you need to ask here, to fully understand the impact of an affliction.

- What is the impact on you, and your company, if you DO reach this goal?

- What is the impact on you, and your company, if you DO NOT?

Can you see that by asking these two questions, the sales person described earlier would not have written a proposal.

And nobody likes writing proposals, at least no one that I know.

There is another benefit, you will probably discover, by asking these two questions about each of the issues you are discussing with your prospect. You should discover some of the personal wins your prospect will receive by resolving these issues.

And don't forget, personal issues are much more important to your prospect than the business problems. The business problems are important, but the personal issues and resolution are much more important to him.

As you can see, you need to uncover the impact your solution will have, not only on your prospect's company, but more importantly, what impact it will have on him personally.

Meaning

Here is where you can give your presentation on your products/services, because now you know your prospects goals, his afflictions, and the impact all of these things will have on him and his company, whether he commits to his goals, and solves his issues or not. And you also know what order everything will occur.

So how do you do this?

You have to pick the value of your products and services that relate to each of his top three goals and resultant issues. But, do not dwell on the features of your product or services. Ensure you show how these features relate to his goals and issues. Relate the features by talking about the value he will receive from buying your products/services.

And I cannot emphasize this enough. Only talk about the value of your features and benefits that relate to his goals and issues, and how he will reach his goals and resolve his issues, with your products and services.

Find a way to demonstrate the *value* your products and

services will bring him. There is an old saying that I like. *Keep your products (and services) behind your back.*

Remember that your prospect really doesn't care how many awards you have won, he only cares about how you can help him realize his goals, and resolve his afflictions.

So, always, always, keep this in mind when you are presenting your solution.

And always get to NO, before you get to YES, so you save yourself, and your prospect, a lot of time.

The GAIM Plan is the sure-fire way to qualify a prospect or client, to see whether you should move forward with him or not.

About Ian Dainty

Ian Dainty's business career began with IBM Canada in 1974 as a B2B sales rep, selling large systems to the financial community. Since 1980, Ian has started and grown three companies, always helping his clients succeed through better B2B marketing and sales strategies and tactics.

Before getting into coaching, Ian owned and operated two B2B technology related businesses. Both companies were software and service related businesses, and very marketing and sales oriented. Ian sold both of them successfully.

Some results Ian has achieved for his B2B coaching clients.

- Helped clients with their sales/marketing initiatives, to help them increase revenues 25% to 100% in one year, and often, two to three times in three years.
- Developed, sold and delivered training and coaching to thousands of B2B sales and marketing people, and executives. Results included helping clients open new accounts, establish executive contact, and increase their Strategic Account Management skills. Ian's training and coaching has generated millions of dollars of revenue for his clients.
- Recently, Ian helped one client triple its client base in just over one year.

Ian has done many things to help his B2B clients grow and succeed.

Website: www.maximizebusinessmarketing.com
Blog: www.maximizebusinessmarketing.com/blog
LinkedIn: https://www.linkedin.com/in/iandainty/
Twitter: https://twitter.com/iandainty
eBook – ENGAGEMENT – B2B Selling in Today's Connected World -
http://bit.ly/B2BEngagement

Bedroom To Boardroom

Mo Bro's founders Keval Dattani, Kunal Dattani and Savan Dattani

Succeeding in ecommerce

When we looked at our roots to market for *Mo Bro's,* we felt that e-commerce was a great fit. The core benefit here was that we were able to get to market quickly. It also allowed us to stay bootstrapped and lean with our overheads. We feel this is vital whilst taking your first brave and bold steps.

The beauty of having an online business is that it allows entrepreneurs to test their ideas with very little investment and have access to millions of customers. It also allows individuals to build a lifestyle of their choosing.

If you have a proven product that solves a meaningful problem, you are already on the path to success.

Your product can be very quickly tested on online marketplaces. You can test price points vs. cost of sales, demand and feedback and proceed onwards and upwards in a short period of time.

If you want to turn your ecommerce store into a successful business, the only thing getting in the way is yourself.

The potential is always present but the entrepreneur has to make the decision to put in the time and effort it requires to scale up.

I get asked many times about my secrets for running a successful ecommerce business. I don't think there are any.

It's possible for anyone to achieve what we have.

One of the biggest attributes we have is the power of three. We are three brothers with different thought processes and skill sets.

As a sole trader, business can be very lonely. You can spend a lot of time unsure if you are making the right decision. The combination of two individuals, on the other hand, presents the problem of whose decision to follow if you're not on the same wavelength. With a team of three, you have the majority vote. Having three minds to weigh-up the pros and cons and the ability to settle on what two members of the team agree on speeds up the decision-making process.

Identifying your customers

When starting a business it's essential that you know who your target customers are.

Once you've started trading, it's important to start mapping out your target audience — finding out what they like and dislike about your products so you can improve.

Think of Apple when it released the first device. It wasn't perfect, nothing ever is. But they started with a version one and improved based on customer feedback. You need to apply this to your product or business. Learning from what works and what doesn't will have a direct impact or your sales going forward.

I've spoken to many businesses that don't take customer insight seriously. I can kind of understand it. After all, who knows your product better than you? But it's also an amateur mistake.

By identifying your key demographics, you can concentrate your efforts on marketing to a warm audience, rather than people who are not interested. Think of it as a lot of wasted time which becomes more valuable as you start to develop in business. Time is one thing that we can never buy or get back.

Marketing on the right channels

When *Mo Bro's* began trading, we began by promoting on social media, however, that got us nowhere fast.

Our best results came when we started looking for other platforms. First *eBay* and then *Amazon*. Doing this allowed us to double our turnover within the first 12 months.

These platforms also allowed us to identify that our products were more than just a consumable. We were selling 600% more products during holiday seasons, which meant beard care was fit for gifting. We used this information and began creating gift kits. Today, these kits stand as our core offering.

So, understanding your customer and marketplace is key. It was one of the core catalysts for our early success.

Of course, this doesn't mean that your business will map out the same way, but it's an example of finding what your business is centred on: *who is your target market and what products do they want?*

Take this principle seriously and you'll be able to figure out where to spend your marketing budget for the best return on investment. You'll find it much easier to bring in a steady stream of leads.

To help identify your target market you need to be able to answer the following questions:

- Who would pay for my product or service?
- Who has already bought from you?
- What does your own network think?
- What is your revenue model?
- How will you sell your product?
- How did your competitors start?
- How will you find customers?
- What is the current marketplace saturation?
- What are your core unique selling propositions?

Customers as brand ambassadors

Another success we've had at *Mo Bro's* is using customers as brand ambassadors. You can be as passionate and as vocal as you like about your products but it will never speak as loud as a glowing review or testimonial from a customer.

There is no substitute for word of mouth. Make it as easy as possible for customers to compile and share reviews.

Your customers are your greatest asset and what they say has the biggest impact on sales and on your buying decisions.

Creating a website

Starting out on marketplaces like *eBay* and *Amazon* is a great way to learn about your customers and scale your business quickly but once you're established you should think about investing profits in your own website. Your website is where you can really start to build your own business as you're creating a marketplace of your own.

Having a website means you're no longer competing with dozens of other sellers offering the same product. Naturally, this means customer loyalty is far higher. We retain 44% of all customers on the *Mo Bro's* website, which is high for our industry.

A website also gives you the change to consider the true value of each customer and use marketing insights to work out their lifetime spend, *average order value* (AOV), units per transaction, *click-through rate* (CTR) and conversion rate.

By digging into your marketing analytics, you can gain a good insight into your *cost per acquisition* (CPA) and use the data to gain new customers from social advertising and platforms such as *Google AdWords*.

At *Mo Bro's*, we always aim for at least break-even on the first purchase. However, I've seen some sales models that work at a loss. Some of the best e-commerce businesses I have come across are modelled to create an eco-system. A perfect example of this are subscription services that will give you the first pack for free in the knowledge that they will retain customers for an average of 4-5 orders. Orders 2-3 often are break even and into profit.

The importance of consumer behaviour

Industry data suggests that consumers look at between four and eleven other websites, including your competitors, before making a purchase, there are number of factors involved in making that decision which you should consider.

To strengthen your position in the mind of the consumer, your marketing strategy should have multiple touch points so that you're able to remain visible even when the customer isn't on your website. There are many tools for this, the most popular being social remarketing, web retargeting, and *Google* display and *Google Shopping*.

It's also important to understand that consumers never want to be directly sold to. You need to make sure you can offer value before any purchase is made. This can be industry leading blog posts or content that helps educate them.

It could be a *product for a prospect* such as a free download or sample that your competitors are not offering. These things might not clinch a sale in the first instance, but having consumer sign up to your email database means you have a second chance at getting in touch with them.

Stay in the consumer's eye so that, when the time is right, they can return.

Streamlining the sales process

Making it easier for consumers to buy from your site when the time is right is so important. Most people these days do not have the time or patience for something that doesn't work or takes longer than it should, so you should avoid over-complicated sales processes. If you want to sell more products, you must make sure your visitors are not getting frustrated and leaving your site to find another store.

There are a few steps to consider here. I would recommend having a simple checkout that appeals to the less savvy online shoppers. Make sure that you are covering all of the popular payment options such as *PayPal, Amazon Pay, Stripe, Google Pay* and *Apple*.

Another popular way of streamlining your checkout process is by allowing guest checkouts. However, while this is good for the consumer, it restricts you in terms of the data you can retain.

An increasingly popular workaround for this is to allow consumers to log in through existing online accounts (e.g. *Gmail* and *Facebook)*. This is the perfect middle ground as you manage to capture some details and give customers options that they know and trust.

Consider having your checkout automatically save billing and payment information for customers to make future purchases quicker. Making minor tweaks like changing your default shipping option to the cheapest can increase sales conversions instantly.

We use a tool called *Hotjar* that allows us to record website customer behaviours. This information can be used to see where your customer may be getting frustrated and will help you identify drop offs or errors in your sales funnel. Our best advice is to only make a single change at any given time, so you can measure the direct impact of that change on your site

Business software

Paper notes and *Excel* documents are fine in the early days of business, but as things grow you'll start to find yourself getting bogged down in admin tasks that take away from things you should be doing to increase sales. To overcome this issue, there are numerous business tools to help improve day-to-day running by helping to manage stock, order and fulfilment management, and marketing.

Given the variety of tools available, make sure that any system you choose is suited to your business and matches all your requirements. It's important to do your groundwork.

Research and identify your challenges and set dates to re-evaluate tools on a six-month basis to make sure they are performing as they should. I would consider cost vs. longevity (future proofing) and function. A good system will form a part of your foundation and will become an asset.

The best e-commerce businesses I have seen are those that evolve and adapt to the latest developments in technology. Keep a close eye on your marketplace — be dynamic and reactive.

Just remember it's okay to change lanes but never paths.

Be an expert in your field.

About the Mo Bros

Keval, Kunal and Savan Dattani a trio of British-based entrepreneurs. Brothers, they are CEOs/co-founders of *Mo Bro's* — the UK's leading men's grooming retailer, specialising in beards and moustaches. Since 2014, the band of brothers have helped over 300,000 bearded brethren in 78 countries enjoy better beards.

Within three years, *Mo Bro's* have excelled in e-commerce, and have achieved viral status exceeding 125 million global views. The brand are duty-free suppliers to major airlines and cruise liners. *Mo Bro's* have been featured nationally in *The Telegraph, Express, Enterprise Nation, Business Advice, Metro* and BBC *Dragons' Den*. They are also crowned as *Export Champions* by the Department of International Trade and are fronting their national *Exporting is Great* Campaign.

The *Mo Bro's* brand has been recognised with industry awards for *Leicester Mercury Retailer of the Year, Niche Magazine Best Business Growth* and *Natwest Great British Entrepreneur Awards* and many more.

The American author, Rolf Smith, once said that *"great ideas can come from anywhere, at any time."* This was certainly the case when the brothers decided to take part in growing their facial hair for charity back in 2014. Little did they know that a short time down the line they'd be giving up their day jobs for a career in men's grooming. "If you told us at the start of the *Movember* challenge that soon we'd be turning a £750 investment into a seven-figure business with no debtors, we'd have laughed in your face. But when it became apparent that an online male grooming brand is something we could make work, we were in no doubt that we'd succeed."

www.mobros.co.uk
@mobrosgrooming
hello@mobros.co.uk

7 High Impact Strategies To Build Successful Lasting Relationships - The Empathic Approach To Selling Profitably

Susan Marot

In today's competitive market, it can be difficult to make a first impression on a client let alone build a long-lasting relationship with them. However, if you don't build a solid working relationship faster than Usain Bolt can run the 100m, your customer will be soon be doing business with a shiny new competitor who has promised to not only serve up the moon, but the sun and stars too!

There is so much choice for clients and in many markets, there is little to distinguish the big players. Coupled with it being a lot easier to change suppliers than it ever used to be and the constant pressure to also close profitable new business, sales people seem to have an even tougher job keeping clients.

Successful business relationships are at the heart of profitable companies. From internal working relationships with colleagues to those with external partners, everyone has a part to play in maintaining a profitable balance. However, it is those in sales that play the most important role of all.

Let's be very clear about three things.

- Sales people bring cash into a business.
- People buy from people.

- Client relationships will always affect the bottom line.

Therefore, building and winning long lasting relationships simply has to be a priority for every sales person.

Even before you meet your future client, the task of building that relationship has started. Then when the client is won, the very best sales people don't move onto the next hot prospect. They tend that client like a delicate, newly planted sapling blowing in the wind.

So, what can you do before, during and after you win new clients to turn them into lasting, profitable relationships.

1. Research for hidden gems

Getting the conversation started with prospective clients can often be a challenge. Face to face meetings aren't too bad as we can always default to state of the weather or the big game at the weekend. Having said that idle chit chat is OK for the walk from reception down to the buyer's office, but how do you successfully turn that into a meaningful business conversation?

Even more of a challenge is starting the conversation using only the written word via social media or email. If you can actually get the words in front of the decision maker, how do you start to make a big impression?

This is where research really comes into play. Yes, take a look at their website to see what their company is saying about themselves, but why not carry out a few different *Google* searches as well. This will throw up the opinions of others and what they think about your prospect or company. Look at the market and industry sector they operate in. What are the big stories that could affect their world and possibly yours?

Take a business who heavily relies on road transport to deliver its goods. What if the price of fuel goes up and consider what the consequences of that might be to them. Think about any connections between what is currently important to them right now, and how that could relate to your product or service.

Remember: *Fail to prepare. Prepare to fail.*

2. Be creative with your introductions

We all know that you don't get a second chance to make a first impression, so think about how you could go about this differently to the competition. Social media platforms such as *LinkedIn* are great tools for approaching new clients, but they are popular and overcrowded too.

For me the best way to make a high impact introduction is to get in front of them. This can be a challenge, which is why sales people need to think outside of the box to come up with a solution.

A few years ago, I sold operational software to the UK Police. The ultimate decision would land on the desk of a high-ranking officer, who was always more interested in solving the latest murder than meeting an IT sales woman.

After some thought, I decided to try a different approach and attended a public Police Board meeting. I was the only member of the public sat in a row of empty seats, so I stood out like a sore thumb. As was my right I was asked if I had any questions of the board and took the opportunity to ask a funding question because I knew they had a hole in the budget. When the meeting turned private I was asked to leave. However, I knew the decision maker would remember me.

The following week I contacted the PA to the decision maker, saying I had attended the meeting and as a result I had come up with a possible solution to help solve their budget issue.

Bingo! I got the meeting and a great client relationship was formed. In fact, I still remain in contact with that senior officer today.

If the result of a little bit more creativity means you can make a bigger impact, then you have nothing to lose and everything to gain.

3. Increase your empathic curiosity

As sales people, we understand the importance of uncovering our client's problems, needs, wants and desires. If not, then we will simply fail to close the deal, as it is near impossible to sell a solution without first finding the problem.

Empathic curiosity during the sales process will help sales people to qualify and quantify the opportunity. However in reality, it is a style that is rarely demonstrated in B2B sales.

To better explain, I would like to share philosopher Roman Krznaric's meaning of empathy.

"Empathy is the art of stepping imaginatively into the shoes of another person, understanding their feelings and perspectives and using that to guide your actions."

Krznaric. R. (2014). *Empathy: Why It Matters, And How To Get It*. Rider, an imprint of Ebury Publishing.

In this fascinating book, Krznairic highlights six habits of empathic people of which one of those is to practice the craft of conversation. He then goes through the 6 elements within the craft of conversation.

- Curiosity about strangers
- Radical listening
- Removing your mask
- Concern for the other
- A creative spirit
- Sheer courage

By increasing your empathic curiosity above and beyond just questioning and listening sales techniques, you will discover the ability to truly deep dive into another level of customer relationship. Krznairic warns of using these elements as a must follow step by step process or set of techniques. Though I believe with substantial conversation practice, sales people can develop a more successful level of emphatic curiosity during the questioning phase of the sales process.

4. Adopt a push not pull approach

No one likes to be pushed or rushed into any kind of decision. In my experience, women can be especially good at pulling a positive response from someone, given the time to do so using empathic techniques.

Allowing your customer sufficient time to think about the decision to buy is incredibly important to the success of the deal. Don't get me wrong. You shouldn't just leave the decision in your buyers control to tell you when they are ready, but you don't need to chase after them.

My golden tip is to ask the buyer when they are happy for you to contact them to find out their decision. This technique ensures the buyer feels in control, but keeps you at the fore front of their mind.

5. Be helpful, but not generous

"I was wondering if you could help me at all?"

This must be the one phrase I have said more than any other in my very long sales career. I mean, who can resist anyone who offers assistance?

It's the one question I use every time I speak to a gatekeeper. Gatekeepers are naturally helpers by nature, it's their job and it helps them to quickly warm to you.

It is incredibly important to see the gatekeeper as someone who can help you. They are not someone to be pushed aside as you aim for the dizzy heights of speaking to the decision maker.

Try to use helpful positive terms throughout the sales whole process and with everyone you meet. This is about appearing humble, but entirely professional as you demonstrate your clear intent to reach a win/win scenario for both the buyer and yourself.

6. Challenge when appropriate

It is your duty to make sure your prospects feel that they got a cracking deal. However, at the same time you need to make it clear that you aren't a walk over either. Your clients overall are reasonable people, but like you they are also under pressure to get the right deal.

Imagine being faced with working through the night to come up with a revised proposal because the client hits you with a curve ball, but they need an answer by nine the following morning. Be honest and say if that it isn't possible.

Or how about when the competitor presents a ridiculously low price, which there is no way you can beat. If that is the case then don't be nervous, just say "We stand firm on our price, because we know we can address all your needs, and much more beside".

These types of sales situations are tough, but sometimes your client just needs to feel that they worked hard to achieve a great deal for their company too. When both sides consider they have achieved something good, then there is definitely a sense of trust on both sides that they can do that again and again.

7. Keep your word

Trust is essential for any successful business relationship. If you are saying you are going to do something for your client, then make sure you do. If for some unfortunate reason you can't, then own up as quickly as possible.

It doesn't matter if things go wrong during the sales process. In fact, it is often a good thing when problems occur.

Overcoming a difficult situation for your client proves that you have their best interest at heart and that is a difficult point for them to ignore.

Just be swift in your actions, keep them informed, and lastly ask if you have resolved the issue to their complete satisfaction. Remember problems can be an opportunity to build on the relationship, not torpedo it.

Finally, keep empathy at the heart of every part of your sales process. When you consistently put yourself in your customer's shoes, you will undoubtedly have a customer base build on solid, profitable relationships for both you and your clients business.

About Susan Marot

For over 30 years, Susan Marot has had an undeniable passion for selling successfully. Across the UK and Europe, she still continues to sell to corporations as well as the challenging government sectors. Sharing her expertise in the B2B sales process, coupled with a huge dose of empathy, this customer centric approach is what helps her clients to achieve greater sales success.

Susan is engaged by many companies at the top of their sector to deliver onsite training and coaching. Susan also helps those sales people who don't have access to a supportive sales coach or trainer, through her popular online sales training, or 1-1 online coaching.

Susan Marot believes that once a sales person fully understands the whole sales process and its impact on the prospect, they can then take that approach and successfully apply it to any market or industry sector.

Susan also loves to share her enthusiasm for selling successfully on the big stage. Knowledgeable and entertaining, delegates leave her keynotes feeling energised and enthused to successfully use their newly learnt skills back in their day to day sales life.

https://www.succeedatselling.com
https://www.linkedin.com/in/susanmarot/
https://www.facebook.com/SucceedatSelling/
https://www.pinterest.es/SucceedatSellin/pins/
https://twitter.com/SucceedAtSellin
https://www.instagram.com/succeedatsellingnow/

Why Did We Miss The Sales Target?

Martin Zeman

Business is like Formula 1

Running business is like running a *Formula 1* racing team. We aim to win the championship (exit a business, IPO or become a leader of our industry) by getting together the best team, designing the best cars (products and processes) and racing faster than the competition without crashing.

One of the most important elements in *Formula 1* is the car's engine. In business the engine is Sales and Marketing.

When the engine runs smoothly, everyone is happy.

The problem is when the engine stops performing as expected – i.e. the sales target gets missed.

When a speed dial indicates a car doesn't go as fast as it should the world-class racing teams look at their diagnostics, quickly find out the root cause of the problem, fix it and continue racing.

The same goes for world-class companies. Unfortunately when it comes to sales engines most companies don't have the right diagnostics in place. They all have a speed dial - a report that compares actual revenue with a forecast – so they know when there is an issue. But the report doesn't tell them what's causing the issue or what to do about it. They have to keep on racing with an inefficient engine being at a disadvantage against their competitors.

I love implementing effective sales diagnostics for companies.

Here's how you can set up sales diagnostics in your own company and by doing that increase revenue and profit and improve predictability of your sales.

Why did we miss the sales target?

Is this scenario familiar?

It's the end of a quarter and sales fell short of the target.

A CEO comes to the sales team and asks an obvious question: *"Why did we miss the sales target?"*

Sales team feels under pressure and responds with something like: "No one is buying right now, the economy is slow", "We are too expensive", "We'll surely make up for it next month" or "Marketing doesn't generate enough good leads".

So the CEO goes to the marketing team and asks them the same question: *"Why did we miss the sales target?"*

"Sales team doesn't follow up on our leads", "We don't have enough marketing budget" or "Revenue is not our responsibility, our objective is to generate leads, which we did".

How would you feel if you were that CEO?

Uncertain? Angry? Frustrated? Stressed? Powerless?

None of those would be surprising. But business leaders don't have the luxury to dwell on emotions they have got a business to run and salaries to pay, so they go back to the sales team with a carrot and a stick and they get the sales team to work harder.

However the more we use incentives and threats the less effective they get. If the sales team feels the pressure is on all the time they get exhausted and start leaving. And it's often the best reps that leave first.

And with the best talent leaving, more sales quotas get missed which leads to more pressure on the team and more sales reps leaving - a vicious cycle.

But it doesn't have to be this way! Instead of working harder you could work smarter.

Just consider what would happen if you got the true answer to the question "Why did we miss the sales target?"

What if you knew what the real problem is?

Of course, you would solve it. Business leaders are natural problem solvers. They solve one problem after another. But it's impossible to solve a problem if you don't know what the problem is.

Root cause problems

A missed sales target is a problem but it's just a consequence of underlying problems. Addressing the outcome (making your sales team work harder) may fix the issue temporarily. Resolving the root cause will prevent the consequence from recurring.

Let's lift the bonnet of your car and look at the typical root causes of missed sales targets.

Missing a sales target should never come as a surprise. A prospective buyer's journey is quite predictable and the more prospects you get the more predictable it is.

- From every £100 spent on marketing and advertising you gain a certain number of leads,
- Through lead nurturing process some of these leads turn into opportunities,
- These opportunities are then led through a sales process. And at each step of the process a certain percentage of opportunities moves forward in the process and certain percentage gets lost. Simple.

The common sense suggests that if you feed enough leads into the process, you will get enough revenue out, right?

Not necessarily.

Understanding why and when this is not the case is the key to fixing the effectiveness of your Sales engine.

Here are the two root causes behind the lack of sales.

Lack of accountability for the Marketing team

"Marketing doesn't generate enough good leads" - Sales

In many companies Sales and Marketing are misaligned. Sales' goal is to generate revenue and Marketing aim is to generate the highest number of leads for a given budget.

Where is the problem?

A marketing department whose sole objective is to generate maximum number of leads for a given budget doesn't always care about the quality of their leads.

The goal for Marketing should be similar to that of a Sales team - revenue. Better yet the *return on investment* (ROI) from marketing spend - in other words *"How much money do we get back from every £1 spent on marketing?"*

Marketing might argue that they are not in control of what happens with the leads once they pass them on to the sales team and therefore they shouldn't be held accountable for that. In some companies Marketing can't even see what's happening with their leads in Sales.

Don't let that stop you.

Build a Marketing return on investment (ROI) report.

The ROI report shows how much money has company spent on various channels and campaigns each month and what revenue (or profit) got generated from this spend.

For example the report may show that you've spent £10,000 on *Google AdWords* in May, which generated 100 leads of which 10 became clients with overall gross profit of £15,000 therefore the return on investment is (£15,000 - £10,000) / £10,000 = 50%.

Even if you won't make ROI an official performance metric for Marketing, by making it visible Marketing will naturally start to prioritise investments into the most profitable channels and campaigns.

Lack of accountability for the Sales team

"Sales is not following up on our leads" - Marketing

Sales reps are artists. They often follow their gut feel rather than a structured process. They believe that as long as they deliver their targets they should be left alone. While this works for them it often doesn't work for the company.

Sales reps can easily get excited about a few hot opportunities and focus on them at the expense of other opportunities.

But without the attention prospects lose interest or buy elsewhere. Either way the company loses the opportunity and the potential revenue.

Companies lose a lot of money this way.

Simple solution?

Hold Sales accountable to progress all the opportunities forward in a timely fashion.

Build a Pipeline report.

Pipeline report shows all the open opportunities by stage and how long they have been in that particular stage. For example we can see there are 30 opportunities in a quote stage and five of them haven't been updated (i.e. there was no related activity logged) for more than a month.

The findings from this report are almost always the same. The pipeline itself looks great with lots of opportunities and lot of value inside but when we look at the detail it's clear that many of those opportunities are too old to still be alive.

There might be various reasons for that – maybe sales reps haven't done those activities, maybe they just forgot to update the CRM system, and maybe they left the opportunities open on purpose to make their pipeline look big and healthy.

Whatever the reason transparency will give you a clean true picture of the pipeline and help you identify and prioritise opportunities that need attention.

Obstacles to watch out for

Holding your Marketing accountable for return on their spend and your Sales team accountable for progressing all the opportunities forward will naturally align the two departments.

But beware. When you set out on a journey to make your sales engine transparent you are likely to encounter a couple of obstacles that can hinder your initiative.

Disconnected and poor quality data

Data quality and availability is the biggest obstacle when it comes to data projects.

Data are often incomplete, inaccurate and spread across numerous disconnected systems.

This situation is normal. The issue is not that this is the case but that the expectations about the data quality are unrealistic. It's important to acknowledge that initially companies might not be able to answer all the questions they want because the data is just not available yet.

Some companies try to address this by starting a two-year project to clean up the data and build a sophisticated reporting system only to find out two years later it didn't work.

I strongly recommend going the agile way and deliver value as soon as possible using the data you've got today. This will show people there is value in data and enable you to build up momentum before taking the next steps towards more and better quality data and insights.

Good data projects to start with are:

- Analysis of the most valuable customers,
- Analysis of the most profitable products, and
- Pipeline report (as mentioned above)

Most companies have data for these projects readily available and the insights usually make a big difference.

Whatever report or analysis you start with, expect that initially the information won't be completely accurate. Stay calm and carry on and once you've exposed the data get your teams to clean up the data. Be persistent.

Resistance to change and fear of transparency

Many people don't like change and transparency.

Sales teams in particular are often less enthusiastic about transparent sales engines. They focus on the potential downsides - being more closely managed and having to spend more time updating systems. To get them on board it's important to show them how transparency can actually help make them more money.

One of the best ways to do that is to form a small project

team with one or two representatives from both marketing and sales. Choose individuals who embrace change and who genuinely want to improve your business. Once they have proven the value of the project and once others see their success it will be easier to get the rest of the company on board. With Sales teams often not being the top proponents of the insights projects and due to their strong position in organisations I strongly recommend sales diagnostics projects are led directly by the CEO who has got authority over both Sales and Marketing teams.

In summary

Sales and Marketing is the engine of your company. Knowing why it's performing the way it is, is vital for staying competitive and growing your business.

Sales diagnostics is the key to provide transparency and accountability to your sales process addressing the main root causes of lower than expected sales.

With effective sales diagnostics in place you will never have to ask again *"Why did we miss the sales target?"*

Even when it happens, you will know exactly why and you will be able to fix it quickly and keep on winning your business race.

About Martin Zeman

Martin Zeman is a data consultant and director at *Data Driven Era*. His mission is to change the way companies use data - instead of using it just to inform the business he shows companies how to use it to improve their business.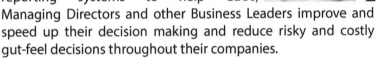

Martin and his team build effective reporting systems to help CEOs, Managing Directors and other Business Leaders improve and speed up their decision making and reduce risky and costly gut-feel decisions throughout their companies.

Their primary focus is Sales and Marketing – the engine of every business.

www.datadrivenera.com
www.linkedin.com/in/martinzeman

Social (Really is...) Selling

Tristan Griffiths

When I tell people I have been in business for over 20 years, the first question I get is usually, *'What face cream do you use?'* – Maybe something I should look into, however that is not the most surprising part for most people of this story.

Having started my own business journey aged just 12, whilst in a private school in London, transforming my £5 pocket money into hundreds per term, I really was doing well in business.

I wasn't caught up on the right terminology, or if I was doing things *the right way*. It was more gut instinct and personal judgment – which clearly paid off well. Until on frightful day when I was summoned to the headmaster's office, with my mother, for a reprimanding.

Luckily my mum was of an entrepreneurial mindset too, and after the very strict South African headmaster had laid it on thick about how dishonest I had been, my mum was sure they were just jealous they weren't getting a cut.

As we left the office that day, she looked down at me and said: *'You're going to do it again aren't you?'* to which I replied *'Yes'.*

What happened next was a defining moment in my business and entrepreneurial journey and one I could never have predicted. Mum looked down at me and said, 'OK – just don't get caught next time.'

Had she chosen to respond differently to my headmaster's outburst, things may have turned out very differently, but they didn't and here we are 24 years on, self employed, delivering regular talks, trainings and mentoring others to excel in their chosen business field.

I am not telling you this to impress you, but more to impress upon you that the decisions we make each day, ultimately shape our futures and the successes we reap in the future

The key takeaway from this early lesson in sales was that people buy from people they know, like, and trust.

That small five pound tuck shop started trading in the hundreds in a very short period of time by leveraging a few key factors that still ring true in my business today:

Know Your Value

Looking around at the retail stores and restaurants closing down, more by the day, it is interesting to think that these were mostly chains that ran promotions and discounts to try and entice customers in.

This is a slippery slope and customers get addicted to discounts. I am sure you, like I have, are guilty of heading to a spot only when the deal is on. After all, why would you go at full price if you know the deal is on so often?

Ask For It

Once you know and appreciate your own value, it then takes skill and courage to ask for what you are worth. But the more you do, the easier it gets - trust me!

Asking for the value you know you are worth is empowering. As soon as you get it, you will wonder why you worked so long for less.

Now back to the main reason I told you the story of the school tuck shop. It was not a cute story and chance to reminisce, but more a framing for what is to come.

Like many things in life, the lessons we learn, equip us to better deal with situations in the future. And as you are reading this I would assume you want to make more sales, so let's get down to it!

Sales Are Simple

There I said it.... But it's true. People often overthink the sales process, and that fundamentally holds them back. There are a few key components but these become more and more predictable the more you study the process.

As long as you have a product of service that people want, then you can make sales. Sometime even if people don't realise or think they want to buy, you can still sell them.

You are the sales person and it's your job, much like my story early on in this chapter, to build rapport with them as quickly as possible. The better you get at this, the more you will sell.

Be Social

I am often asked how I manage to sell so much without really selling.

Again, it's simple... I have spent the past 24 years learning and understanding that people behave in predictable patterns. Once you understand the patterns you can replicate them and tweak them to get the results you want.

I network a lot, and even now run my own networking event, designed to bridge a gap I saw in that market, but I digress. Networking is the perfect opportunity to be social with people, without their normal barriers up, and to get to know one another.

This is the very principle of how you should treat your potential customers.

Invest In Them

It's important to invest time in understanding the customer, and what problems they face, as only then can you even consider providing a solution. And when you realise that is all you are doing, the 'sale' becomes easy.

If you do not pay attention, or miss something during those early conversations with a prospective lead, you may be completely off the mark, so laser focus your attention on them and only them.

Treat them like they are the most important person in the world and every word is crucial to your day.

I know people who have won HUGE deals based on the smallest of details.

For example, upon winning a big contract at tender, when asked if he had any questions, the winner asked, *'Why Me? The others are more established and bigger ... "*

...to which he was surprised to hear that, remembering and going over and above to send a birthday card (something he found normal) was the deal clincher.

Show Value

This comes in two parts.

Value in the product or service goes without saying. The more the person needs or wants it, then the more valuable it appears to them.

However you can show value in other ways too. Taking time to value their time and paying attention to the smaller details will make then feel more comfortable with you, and when they do, and the time is right they will buy from you.

Four Factors of Sales

In any sales situation there are four main factors that need to be considered :

- Right Solution
- Right Person
- Right Timing
- Easy Of Access To Information

Notice that price is not even a factor in this method and therefore you will not be tempted to discount / provide offers.

When you can provide the maximum value and your customers recognise that it's the best solution, then price becomes far less relevant, and they make quicker and more confident purchasing decisions.

My top tips roundup for increasing your sales with ease through social selling:

1. Networking

Go to more events, become know by people who may buy and those who may refer you, and spend time getting to know those people.

These are easy to find from Meetup.com, Eventbrite, Facebook Events, Local Chamber Of Commerce etc.

2. Pay attention

Much more than you think you need to. Make those people feel special and remember more of what they told you, it will be useful later.

If you know you have a poor memory or even if you don't, make notes in your CRM, or even your smartphone notes.

3. Be Patient

Take your time. Those who rush may get a quick sale, but those who wait gain long term customers, bigger spends & advocacy that is worth far more.

People's attention is the key and building trust takes time and effort - but it will come if you apply these principles.

4. Be Social

In person and online, it's important to keep things social, to stay front of mind, and remember the best selling is done by NOT selling.

Both online and off, make sure you are genuinely interested in people and enjoy time with them. People will notice if it's a front!

5. Positioning

If you have done 1-4 then you are already starting to do this, but become the go-to person in your industry and sales will come to you.

STOP SELLING and become the go to person for your industry, or Key Person Of Influence. Since implementing this, I have never sold more than I do now! So give it a go, position yourself well, be social and see what happens.

6. Offer Value

Both in your attention to others and give before asking always, and you won't go far wrong.

Always look at every interaction from the other side FIRST and provide more than you ever ask for. Value is important in building the trust with someone.

7. Do What You Say You'll Do

Always deliver on the promises. Social Selling is built on reputation and it can be gone in a heartbeat. Under promise and over deliver to leave that real WOW factor with every customer.

In today's world - doing what you say you will do is exceptional already, many overpromise and under deliver. Do not fall into that trap, but provide amazing customer service instead. This really will set you apart.

As I said when we opened this chapter, 'Social really is selling.'

SIDE NOTE: If you wanted to check how you do online, *Linkedin* has a tool called the *Social Selling Index* that measures four key areas to see how you are interacting with others. You can find this at *www.linkedin.com/sales/ssi*

You can learn from this and implement it offline as well.

About Tristan Griffiths

Tristan Griffiths is a Digital Media Marketing specialist who reverse engineers success for his clients, always starting with productivity.

An international speaker and training provider, Tristan heads up the agency *ItsNomad9*, that provides innovative content creation & syndication services, as well as account management across a range of industries, globally allowing them to seamlessly learn from each other.

Having successfully build and managed a team of forty 18-24 year old for two years with 100% retention over two years, Tristan is a top social seller, who really knows how to deliver results, whether that is through training, consultation or project management.

With no opportunity left unexplored, Tristan's previous client successes include helping a client make $67,000 on *Snapchat* in just eight weeks, increasing event attendance by 500% and profits by 300% in just three weeks.

And the best bit...

Tristan selfishly wants to help everyone.

ImTristanG.com
Facebook.com/ImTristanG
LinkedIn.com/in/ImTristanG
Snapchat.com/add/ImTristanG
Twitter.com/ImTristanG

Build Your Own System: Create a Monster

Geoff Hetherington

If you want to improve your sales game there are hundreds of systems and training programs available. Some are great, some good and far too many are mediocre.

Of course there are those *'re-badged by a Guru'* ones which are usually no more than a re-working of older established sales techniques that have been dressed up with a new name, and a few buzz words but with no real improvement under the hood. (How many times have you heard *'Remember names, remember faces'*? Or that scarcity sells?)

Each system usually tries to present itself as THE ONE. And if you don't use it you will not be able to achieve the success that is your due! The majority of systems also tend to portray other systems as also-rans or no longer relevant in today's market. As if people have fundamentally changed. (hint they haven't!).

It is a confusing landscape to attempt to navigate so you can improve your selling skills.

I'm not here to sell you a system or even convince you that what I am sharing is the best system or the only method because I don't believe that there is any such thing. Like any other skill that different people have systemised and made into checklists or a methodology one size rarely fits all.

For most of us though, no single system provides all the answers. No off the shelf training will make you a sales success – no matter the promises made.

The truth is that you should seek out a variety of sales training, find the parts of each that resonate with you, those parts that feel natural to use and which garner some actual results. In order to succeed at sales we have to create a hybrid, a monster based on the parts of the systems we have been exposed to that work for us.

Once you have gathered a few bits and pieces that you like from various systems it is time to create your own method. Sit down with a pen and paper, glass of your favourite tipple and map out what your own system will look, feel and sound like. How will you open the sales conversation? Establish rapport? Delve for underlying issues? You need to know the what where and how of what will be your own system.

This is really the old Bruce Lee *'Absorb what is useful'* approach. And it works.

It works because we have differing life experiences, different strengths, weaknesses and biases so the best system for us is the one that we cobble together from exposure to others that is filtered through what get results for us.

Then once we have our monster built we field test it and work to knock off the rough edges and make it smoother, more natural and more a part of us.

Like an actor on stage who learns his lines and then makes them his own during a performance; the modern salesperson has to try a number of systems and then bring together the parts that work for them into a blend of techniques and know how.

I will share my system with you – but it is just that - MY system. It works for me and is the result of several decades of experience, courses undertaken and investigation. It may not work for you but it will give you some pieces to possibly incorporate into your own method of selling.

For the purpose of this article we will take for granted that:

1. You know your Services, Products and client problems inside out.
2. Customers can spot insincerity more easily now than at any other time in history.
3. Sales only happen when there is trust between the customer and the sales person.

4. Trust is built only when the Sales Person has displayed empathy, understanding, appropriate body language and at least some feeling of rapport.

5. You believe that a sale should result in a problem – no matter minor – being solved.

6. You view selling as a form of being of service to your customers and clients.

7. People buy with their emotions but justify with their head in many cases and especially in the case of larger consumer sales.

8. People buy easiest when they are emotionally involved in the sale.

9. They buy least when they let their logical side rule.

10. At their core people buy products or services because of the way they imagine using / receiving them will make them feel.

I work as a Business Advisor, and Coach as well as a Certified Advisory and Governance Board Chair. The core of what I do is solve problems for my clients; and those solutions often require me to sell my clients services, a product or two; or on the need to alter how they view and do things.

I call my own hybrid system the *H3 Method*.

My sales presentations – whether formal or off the cuff – all follow the same sequence of *Heart - Head - Heart*. In other words I work to engage the customers emotions, give some (but not too many) facts, features or benefits and then re-engage their emotions to close.

In order to engage the customers emotions you need to bypass their naturally defensive posture which is head/logic focused. A *Head* focus is analytical and responds to words like *Size, Cost, Price, Money, Extras* and looks for detail.

In the West we are taught to negotiate on price and pretty much price alone, so *Head* questions tend to be all about *Price* and not about *Value*.

Heart on the other hand is about emotion.

It is about the customer imagining how they will feel when they dive into the new pool, win that award or make their first million. It is about the customer seeing a pain relieved a problem solved or a desire met.

Heart is the most powerful determinant of any sale. If I am coaching I use questions like:

- What keeps you awake at 3AM?
- What's working in your business right now?
- How do you feel about that?
- What isn't working?
- Why me? Why now?
- What outcome do you want?
- When do you want it?
- Why is this important to you?
- What will it mean to you and your business if we can fix 'X'?

These needs based questions are designed to get the client thinking about the outcome and the results they want and what it will mean to them. They purposefully do not trigger thoughts or questions about initial costs, how many sessions, who are other clients or the details of how we will work together.

But again they focus on an emotional response.

In a consumer setting I have found the easiest way to engage emotions is to use one of the following three phrases:

- 'Imagine if...'
- 'Let me tell about a time when...' or
- 'Let me tell you a story...'

The story approach is the most powerful because for most of us it holds a strong echo of being a child and Mum or Dad reading to us at bedtime. It triggers a more emotive response. It disarms us and opens up a more receptive, less combative frame of mind. The logical *'just the facts'* part of the mind is pushed to the back...

Like any good story you need a beginning, a middle and an end. In this case the beginning is getting the client to image how they will feel about service of product X. The middle is helping them check off the logical side questions and the end is a return to how they feel when they use the thing you have offered them...

You must finish up with a return to the story to re-engage their emotions of the *Head* becomes dominant again.

Here is an example of a simple consumer story format that I have used:

Heart

Imagine this… it is a hot summer's day, the sun is shining and you're driving along the *Great Ocean Road*, not another car in sight…

The roof is down on your cherry red *Porsche Boxster 718* and *Bon Jovi* is rocking from the speakers…

The sky is a clear blue with a couple of fluffy white clouds and as the wind whips past you catch a salt whiff of the ocean as it breaks onto the sparkling white sand of the beach on your left. You see a few seagulls hovering and some surfer's riding high… it is a perfect Summer's day…

Head

And you get to experience it all because you know that your new car is the perfect one for driving like this on summer days. It rumbles with plenty of power – you know it can do 275km per hour (even if you'll never use it)…and it accelerates from 0 – 100km in 5 seconds and still uses less that 7 litres of petrol every 100kms…and it costs less than you thought possible…

Heart

But nothing, nothing beats the feeling of putting your foot down and hearing the engine growl as you continue that Summer drive along the *Great Ocean Road* ….

Of course this approach may not work for you – but it has for me.

The point here is that I find using the *H3Method* delivers results for me and for some others that I have taught it to. But each of these others added it to or took a part from it for their own systems.

You need to explore and then create your own hybrid, your own *Frankenstein's Monster* of a sales system.

One that is and that works for you.

People in general are not good at making buying decisions – this is why we need guidance and support from smart sales people. And the smartest have built their own *Monster*.

What will yours look like?

About Geoff Hetherington

Geoff Hetherington is an energetic, internationally experienced senior executive with over 30 years' experience as a C Suite Executive across several industries and companies.

Pragmatic Strategy, Penetrating Clarity, Entrepreneurship, Training and Business are particular passions.

Geoff is a Certified Advisory Board Chair; has been a National Award-Winning Marketer, a CEO of businesses in Australia and Asia; and actively involved in the growth, marketing and development of several iconic Australian businesses.

Geoff's skillset encompasses a diverse set of management disciplines such as Strategy Development and Tactical implementation, Entrepreneurialism, Change Management, Project Management; Training Program design and delivery, Corporate Governance, Business Continuity Planning, Sales, Marketing, Retail Operations, and People Management.

A hallmark of his expertise is a focus on pragmatic, effective & efficient strategies with the right tactics to deliver the desired results of his clients.

Geoff works with Boards, Business Owners and Executives to pinpoint where a business is today on a range of issues, helps plot the course to where they want to be in 12 or 36 months' time; then works side by side to deliver the necessary skills, find the right resources and develop the internal capability so that their plans become reality.

In essence - Geoff is a deep generalist and industry agnostic whose specialty is being able to make any business better.

www.theclarityCEO.com ; www.elitebusinessinstitute.com
Linked In: https://www.linkedin.com/in/geoffhetherington/
Email: geoff@theclarityceo.com

Survive and Thrive –
7 Behaviours For Sales Success

Steven Shove, MBA, DipM

Introduction

It was on a cold winter's morning when I awoke to find my shelter covered in snow and a weather system changing towards sleet as I headed towards the camp fire driven by a biting wind. It was in this moment, as a regional Vice-President of sales and as a trainee survival instructor that I realised exactly what it took to survive and thrive in the wild, in life and in sales - to perform to outstanding levels of achievement and with a degree of consistency second to none.

You see, I had been reflecting for a while on the traits of my top sales performers and had been comparing them to the traits of people who had learned to survive and thrive in the wild, which is arguably the most competitive of all environments, from the earliest hunter-gatherers, through each successive period of human development and success right through to modern times.

And my conclusions?

That nothing has changed, the rules of success are the same, that we are born to succeed and that we all have an inbuilt ability to thrive. Whether a hunter or gatherer in sales or a hunter or gatherer in the forest, the rules are the same!

"If you can survive and thrive in the wild with few or

apparently no resources (which you can!), then you can certainly survive and thrive in sales!"

Learning to survive in nature had taught me that we had made our modern and professional lives far too complicated and that we had lost touch with the basics.

By doing so, sales teams, businesses, people and society in general were living lives full of uncertainty. Not only was performance suffering but people's wellbeing too. This was only too apparent to me as I had seen burnout amongst sales professionals that had disrupted and even ended lives.

I resolved that if I could share the lessons learned, then I would be able to make a positive impact on sales performance, wider business performance and the precious people involved in these enterprises too. And this is what I will begin to share with you in the paragraphs that follow.

Look at any high achiever and you will note seven key behaviours that contribute to their success. Successful sales people have always:

- **U**nderstood, connected and engaged with their environment
- **T**argeted and planned well
- **O**rganised themselves, resources and others brilliantly
- **P**rogressed without unnecessary delay
- **I**mproved, innovated and adapted
- **A**chieved their desired results on purpose and with great efficiency, and
- **N**urtured and protected what is important

Understand, connect and engage

Poor and average sales performers will at best *understand* their environment.

They may achieve this by reading materials provided to them by their company, relying on past experiences, researching on the Internet or even deploying specialist business information tools designed to give insight to companies, markets, executives, news and financials etc.

Indeed, I spent much of my own sales career selling such information services. However, doing your homework like this is simply not enough if you wish to enjoy outstanding and more consistently achieved results. The best sales people also connect and engage!

They connect and engage through social media and in person, add value by contributing views, knowledge and ideas, build reputations as key people of influence who can be trusted and to whom people will come for advice.

The result is that the sales professional can influence their environment – their client or prospect base, the competitive landscape, product or industry directions etc. and will therefore benefit from greater created opportunity and first mover advantage.

My best performers networked heavily in their clients' industries e.g. law and insurance and enjoyed serious competitive advantages as they helped these industries to develop new products and ideas that needed our services too.

Through engagement, opportunities are created, and competitive advantage achieved. In the wild, working with the resources around you turns an otherwise barren looking territory into one of abundance, full of foods, medicines, tools and equipment to make your life safe and comfortable. Historically, these skills were not taught but came about through personal engagement and experimentation. Those who complained of lack perished. Those who chose to engage in their territories thrived. And so it is for sales people!

Target and plan

Targeting and planning well sound like obvious requirements for sales success yet so many sales people do this with highly variable degrees of effectiveness, perhaps getting bogged down in their territory plan or one account plan over another, but then ignoring the internal resource requirements needed to win a deal or forgetting to properly plan for an important sales call for example. To avoid this and get clarity as to what needs to be done, a simple review can be made.

I recommend a sales person reviews the following equation:

$$S=f(RTxQ)C$$

In summary, *sales success* (S) is a *function of* (f) doing the *right things* (RT) the *right number of times* (Q), *consistently* (C).

Ask, what are the right things? How often should I do them? How can I build in consistency to my routine? And then do it! I recommend reviewing results and modifying behaviours accordingly until the sales professional sees the results they desire. Sales leaders should coach and measure results.

I shall never forget the immense discipline and routine of my highest ever achieving sales representative. He followed the sales success equation so well I could almost set my watch by his actions on any one day or time of the week. His results were astounding as he ensured that his pipeline remained healthy, that deals progressed well and that his accounts and contacts were nurtured.

In the wild, survival priorities can be a matter of life and death. So too can they be for the sales person, for without the security of knowing they can deliver this can lead to insecurity, anxiety and a downward spiral in performance. Not good for the individual or the company. Sales leaders have a responsibility to help their staff know what needs to be done, how and when to do it. The use of non-onerous, well designed CRM and reporting systems with strong coaching practices can make all the difference.

Organise and prioritise

In sales, there are broadly three things that need to be organised; yourself, your resources and other people.

As a sales leader I am both inspired and frustrated by the *maverick* top performer. Inspired by their sometimes-incredible sales results but frustrated by the trails of unnecessary work left behind for others to do for them, that in turn can damage performance on other teams or in other areas of the business. I refer to this as *the hidden costs of sales*. Helping a maverick to better organise and collaborate can have a huge impact on sales results.

Conversely, I see those struggling to hit target who are poorly disciplined with their time and behaviours or who fail to leverage the correct resources to progress and win an important deal. I recommend sales teams brain storm best personal disciplines, gain clarity on when and how to best secure pre-sales resources and when and how best to manage the wider resources and network of their own company and partner organisations. If a sales leader can support his or her best performers, and especially the mavericks, with systems, team skills, training and processes that do not slow them down, then overall sales and wider business performance can only prosper.

When on expedition to the Arctic, organisation of oneself, one's equipment and the team is key. You would not set out otherwise. Why should this be any different in business?

Before heading into the wilds everything is checked, systems and protocols are agreed, and each team member is trained in his or her disciplines. This make all the difference and makes sure everyone gets back home safely.

Progress without unnecessary delay

Opportunity creation, deal progression and deal closure each need to be achieved with an appropriate level of consistency and volume yet with some sales people it is often the case that various stages of the sales cycle are delayed.

A lack of organisation and personal discipline may often be the cause, but the most frustrating circumstance is when a sales person has done all the hard work and has not had the courage to ask for the business. They have been afraid to do so for fear of the word *"no"*, only to have served up the opportunity to their competitor on a silver platter.

Ask for the business and seek to progress each deal at every possible juncture! Do not be afraid! You may be very pleasantly surprised!

Would a hunter delay the pursuit of its prey in a desert full of hyenas? I think not.

Improve, innovate and adapt

Some sales cycles and client relationships are incredibly complex or exist in situations and circumstances that are continually changing.

Top performers recognise this. They know it too, because they not only understand but are fully engaged with their customer or prospect and their marketplace. They are therefore on the front foot when it comes to the need to innovate, adapt or change their solution or approach. They are open to new ideas and even to radical changes to win and retain important business.

I've known sales people fight and argue for new product developments internally and won, sometimes changing their own company's strategic direction. This benefitted them, their clients and organisation and even changed the standards of their client's industry. Others created entirely new commercial models to secure a foothold in a new account.

Being prepared to adapt and change their approaches and being bold enough to do so made all the difference.

People are the greatest of innovators. In a world and time where there was no security, our species overcame the most tremendous odds as we sought to leave the homelands of Africa and venture towards the north and the retreating glaciers. Our ability to turn sticks into spear throwers and to explore new means of hunting and eventually farming changed human-kind forever. From a few thousand people to over seven billion, our ability to adapt is extraordinary! Use it!

Achieve on purpose

Achieving on purpose and with a sense of efficiency is another key trait of top sales performers. They are not easily distracted, have a very clear direction of what they want to achieve and how to get there and can answer with tremendous clarity as to how far they are along towards achieving their goal. They hold themselves accountable and put simple measures and objectives in place to ensure the nature and volume of activity is sufficient to succeed.

They also seek support from others to help them really know where they are and how to proceed.

They work with efficiency by asking the question, *"Is this adding value to my goal?"* and by avoiding any distractions on tasks that do not.

There is no excuse to not knowing where you are and if you are on track.

The horsemen and women of the Ottoman empire navigated great featureless steppes by using a piece of wood, leather and stick to navigate by the sun. They only had to glance down at their sun compass to know exactly where they were headed and without stopping, know how far they had to go. Find ways to measure and track your progress, but do not let the process slow you down!

Nurture and protect

The very best sales performers always seek to nurture and protect what is important and have a very clear idea on what this means and how to achieve it. For the individual sales representative this translates into taking great care of any qualified prospect or customer, ensuring that deal progress is secured with timely and considered follow up, engagement and pro-active support. It means that networks and relationships are nurtured both internally and externally and it means looking after oneself; physically, emotionally and educationally.

Sales leaders have a duty of care to ensure each of the above is done. They need to secure the systems, behaviours and practices that will ensure the ongoing operational effectiveness and wellbeing of their staff. The latter needs careful attention!

How do business practices, your own sales culture and attitudes towards supporting excellent physical and mental health ensure your team will be there and able to deliver for the business with reliability into the future?

Celebrate and next

And finally, there is an eighth trait of great sales success, that of *"celebration and next"*. The best sales people have always celebrated their wins, they have always reviewed and learned from their losses, but they have never stopped to lose momentum. By continuing towards the next deal, they stayed in the game, remained mentally alert and kept those all so important levels of consistent activity alive to enjoy consistently outstanding results.

In January 2018, a team called the Ice Maidens became the first all-female team to cross Antarctica. It was only by carrying on, even with the smallest and most mundane of tasks that they achieved their goal.

By following the *UTOPIAN*™ process as a prompt and guide to other best practices in your organisation, it is my hope that you also enjoy the benefits of outstanding sales performance that is more consistently achieved.

There is a great deal more to cover, but I hope this has helped you think about how you and your teams are working as a first step to really thriving in sales and personal performance.

About Steven Shove

Steven is an experienced business leader, sales and performance coach, a respected thought leader and one of the UK's most highly qualified survival instructors who passionately applies the principles of *original human success*™ to businesses, teams and individuals seeking to thrive in today's ever demanding and increasingly competitive environments.

For nearly 30 years, Steven consulted to and successfully led a variety of international teams and businesses, improving performance across the myriad of business functions and industries but specialising in sales, business strategy and personal development.

Steven is CEO and Founding Director of the *Really Wild Group* that offers performance improvement coaching and consulting services, inspirational events and executive retreats to the business, education and leisure sectors.

Under his leadership, the team deploys a powerful and proven methodology for success that uniquely equips and enables all business functions and staff at every level to deliver superior performance with far greater consistency and predictability - in the most exciting, engaging and memorable of ways.

Today, Steven works with clients from the boardroom or classroom to the wilds of the Arctic and Borneo.

www.reallywildeducation.com
www.reallywildbusiness.com
LinkedIN: Steven Shove
Facebook: Steven Shove and Really Wild Education

The Unconventional Salesman

James Ker-Reid

I've always been a maverick and unconventional guy that loves challenging accepted customs and norms. When I was at school I was obsessed with looking at ways to break rules and then finding ways to avoid punishment by understanding and exploiting the gaps in the school system. My behaviour led me to better understand the structures, processes and ways to have maximum impact with minimum effort.

When I first started in Sales just after the crash in 2008/09, I realised that the same inefficiencies seen at school also existed within large corporations too.

There are a lot of similarities – both companies and schools need to produce results on a large scale, protect the hierarchy/management and both breed a culture of success at all costs. It's this fascination with systems and hierarchies that led me to think differently about sales and realise that the conventional career path would not be the best way for me.

Upon starting my sales career, I quickly realised that no one was going to teach me the fundamentals of B2B sales, the value of it, or even how to be successful at sales. This has been my quest and passion for the last 10 years – to find new ways to accelerate B2B sales success so that everyone, whether you are new to sales, you're a sales manager or you're an established Director of Sales, can still compete and succeed in this ever-changing world. The world moves so fast and conventional sales practices often do not keep up with this rate of change.

When I was asked to write this piece, I asked my network what they would want to read about in the field of Sales. The overwhelming response was to talk about daily disciplines and practices that can accelerate your sales success. I'm not going to give you another 124-point hit list as these are cheap and aplenty on the internet - you'll end up trying to integrate 124 sales disciplines into your daily life, which is impossible.

In the paragraphs ahead, I wanted to share with you practices that are not frequently spoken about or listed on various forums and many are not seen as synonymous with a sales career. I'll be sharing with you my routines that have worked for me while working in London and in Europe and my hope is that these will be valuable to you whatever location or city you live in.

In each of the areas I'd love to share more with you but with text being my main limitation, I can signpost you to the initial information knowing that your natural curiosity and interest will be peaked to steepen your own learning and of course you can connect with me directly to find out more.

So, what are the key disciplines and practices that you can do to generate momentum in Sales?

1. Create and maintain vitality and health
2. Schedule weekly planning and progress meetings
3. Become a data scientist
4. Think two or three steps ahead
5. Quantify value in real terms
6. Set your own standards
7. Celebrate success consistently

1. Create and maintain vitality and health

This is often an area that is overlooked by salespeople and very few sales managers or CEOs will advise you about health. This is often because they are afraid to reveal their own weaknesses or because they know that they are not practicing a healthy and balanced routine themselves. You have to think of yourself as a professional athlete – you need to eat, drink, practice, perform and win like a gold medallist. It's this commitment that brings some of the greatest results.

Sales is an extremely demanding job with long hours, periods of high activity, periods of excruciatingly detailed and slow work. You'll sometimes end up going to sleep thinking about your numbers, your next deal, your next client meeting, and your upcoming meeting with your boss or business partner. This will put you under huge mental strain.

I've outlined the 'WEEDS' disciplines below to keep you fresh in your sales career:

W - Water - 1 litre before 8:00am
E - Exercise before 7:00am
E - Early starts - on public transport or the road before 8:00am
D - Drafting Days - writing proposals at home or in isolation
S - Salad for lunch

The first two are about getting your body in the right place for a demanding day ahead. Thirdly avoiding the rush hour or heavy traffic with early starts means that you will build mental fortitude and confidence that you'll already have achieved something before someone has their first cup of coffee.

'Drafting days' are to give you the headspace and shut you off to distraction when you need to do deep and meaningful work. And finally salad for lunch will give you the vitality and energy to still concentrate in those afternoon meetings and tasks without suffering from a "carb crash".

2. Schedule weekly planning and progress meetings

In order to feel juiced and ready to take the week by storm, you need to have a strong focus – you should know what your key projects and activities are, and what you will be working on or doing each week. That way you will be able to get to the end of your week and be able to review your impact, accomplishments and key learning experiences.

What are the essential practices for weekly planning and progress meetings?

- Do your weekly planning before the week starts either on Friday afternoon or Sunday night.
- Look one week ahead and see what you need to prepare and plan for.
- Progress meetings: always write down your biggest accomplishments each week in one place so you can look back at how you've come and what progress you've made.

This structure and diligence will give you serious fuel for the journey. It will give you a feeling of gratitude, growth and belief that you are really making progress towards your goals.

3. Become a data scientist

The term *data scientist* wasn't commonplace when I started in sales – *Salesforce CRM* used to have a mere two or three bar charts on a page!

The modern world is rich with data and now we grapple with data overload. I read recently that 2.5 quintillion data points are created each day and, as I write this, 90% of the world's data was created in the last two years.[1]

OK, so what do I mean by a data scientist? Isn't that what Marketing or Sales Operations do?

In order to be successful at sales you need to be thinking two or three steps ahead. Data is your friend in this pursuit. It enables you to spot trends and practices that you didn't know existed and will help you to rectify these practices before the trend becomes harmful.

What are the things you want to be analysing and comparing each month and quarter?

- What is your average deal value? (Pipeline and closed deals)
- What is your pipeline value at each stage?
- How much time are your deals taking within each stage of your sales process?
- Have you been active with all of your deals in the last two weeks? Which deals need attention?
- How many deals are in your pipeline?
- What is your time to close each deal?

- How accurate is your forecasting ability? Do your estimates match the actual date?

These questions will highlight where you have gaps and bottlenecks in your sales process.

4. Think two or three steps ahead

Thinking a few steps ahead should be second nature and is vital for all of your phone calls, meetings and proposals. I often advise our clients to think about their end goal and then work back from there. For example, if you have a phone call with a qualified customer where you want to be able to show them a demo of your product and then submit a winning proposal.

In order to submit a winning proposal you must be able to tell the customer up-front what the next steps are:

"...if you're happy with what you see today we'll arrange a proposal playback call to show you what we've created and to ensure that we're on the right track. If you're happy, we will then complete your proposal and send it to you the following week.

Upon submission, we'll agree on a time for another call or meeting, where we can review your feedback and comments and finalise your proposal. How does that sound?"

It sounds long-winded but this is a salesperson who has a plan for three steps ahead! It's this confidence and control that allows you to create directed and timely momentum in a sales process. It'll also stop you meaninglessly following up with chaser emails.

5. Quantify the value in real terms

There are a lot of salespeople out there who are not sure what their product or service will do for their target customer. If you don't know what it will do or can't estimate what it will do, then you are in the wrong meeting.

You MUST be able to explain and quantify what the value is on each opportunity, purchase and partnership with your clients.

What are you enabling them to do? Why should they be doing business with you?

The value in having this information – referred to as a business case in B2B sales – lies in being able to steer the relevant stakeholders and buyers back to their agreed objectives. This information will help you in the latter stages such as in negotiations when you're explaining the value you've added to the decision maker, buying team or procurement team.

6. Setting your own standards

In Sales, when you start operating at this level and dealing with lots of opportunities, people will begin to begrudge you. You'll be planning your time, focussing on high value activities, analysing your successes and evaluating your pipeline in extraordinary detail; so much so that your colleagues, friends or even your family may change their attitude toward you.

You'll be called names or be described as ruthless, *difficult, demanding, boring* or different – *you're not like us.*

Don't get hung up on this name-calling, it's normal. Name calling is often an expression of the perpetrator's insecurities, so try to be considerate of their feelings, but do not let their words affect you or your work.

You don't need validation from anyone.

7. Celebrate success consistently

Sales can be full of ups and downs so it's doubly important to celebrate your successes. It's the celebration of those little wins that gives you the fuel and desire to go beyond your comfort zone to places that you and your company have never been before.

This is essential in sales.

You will end up using your data and fact-based intelligence to recognise all of the individual successes in your sales role, sales pipeline or business. You'll spot the errors and be able to correct them. You'll see the growth and be able to replicate your formulas.

You'll be able to make an impact and each win will feel incredible!

Here are some of my personal practices for celebrating on a regular basis:

- Arrange at least 1 week off per quarter before it has even started – preempt success.
- Create a 'fun-fund' (bank account) from your commissions to enjoy monthly guilt-free spending.
- Create a never-ending experience hit-list and use your 'fun-fund' to enjoy them fully.

Conclusion

I wanted to share with you my honest understanding of success in sales. I have listed the key disciplines and attitudes that I think are essential for all salespeople to cultivate in order to build a business and reach their goals.

It's often the unconventional and novel ideas that bring you the greatest success. As if it were so easy, why wouldn't everyone else be doing it?

I hope my short summary has been of help and will aid you in your own mission.

I look forward to meeting you and hearing about your successes.

Very best of luck.

About James Ker-Reid CEO, Sales for Startups

James Ker-Reid is a sales hacker and unconventional sales consultant. He brings with him infectious energy, honesty and a desire to make a big difference for his clients. He is the founder of *Sales for Startups*, a company that was formed after the company he previously invested in, *Appirio*, a *Workday* system integrator and *Salesforce* partner, was sold to *Wipro Limited* for $500million in October 2016.

His sales philosophy is to combine enduring sales strategies and tested principles with new technology to scale up success and presence for his clients.

Having learnt all he could from tech and B2B sales, he is now working with technology companies to double their sales revenues in as little as six months. His company, *Sales for Startups*, is known for having achieved this for each of their retained clients.

James's long-term vision is to create the first on-demand sales consultancy for technology companies. This consultancy would cultivate success by combining technology and predictive software to give an immediate response on key variables, whilst still maintaining the human element of business by providing an affordable and on-hand consultant.

www.salesforstartups.co.uk
www.linkedin.com/in/jameskerreid

Fully Booked – How to Sell Your Service and Turn Time into Money

David Rothwell

This is the story of a European airport transfer company, who has grown from start up to scaling their business every year for ten years. They have bought two competitors and subsequently been acquired by an international travel operator. All by successfully advertising online in over 30 countries with *Google Ads* (recently rebranded from *AdWords*).

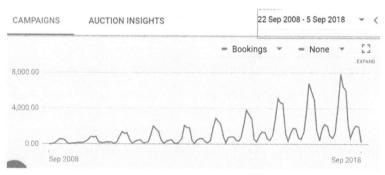

10 years of continual growth

Your time is money

As a service professional, your *product* is time.

If you don't sell it, and continue to sell it, and make more money than you spend in the process, you go broke.

No professional service business wants an empty calendar.

Every service professional selling time wants to be *Fully Booked,* showing up at the right time at the right place, to do your thing and get paid (or having already been paid).

Your calendar needs to fill itself up with self-service bookings. If not, every hour you don't sell your service is gone – forever. You can never get it back or earn the money you lost.

Being *Fully Booked* means you can raise your prices, choose better clients, scale your business, hire more staff, buy more marketing, expand your operation and even make yourself redundant or retired if you want.

"Fully Booked" – how much money is a full calendar worth to you?

Follow the money

For eCommerce merchants and digital sales companies, with a shopping cart and payment processor, it's easy to track money changing hands online, what they spend, how much money they make and how profitable it is. When they do it right and the economics work, campaigns become profit centers with unlimited daily budgets.

But professional service providers sell time for money. Unlike eCommerce and digital sales, with this kind of business it can be more difficult to know if you're even making money, and how much.

Or maybe not …

Think bookings not leads

If you think it's all about getting more leads, for less money, you've completely missed the point. It's not about the leads, it's about what you do with them, and how much they are worth in *Customer Lifetime Value* (CLV). This value tells you the most money you should spend to get them.

Instead of leads, think bookings. Because when you get a lead, what happens next? You still have to contact your prospect, have a conversation with them, find out if you can do business with each other, and move to the next stage. That process is based on an appointment for which you need a self-service online booking.

Don't waste time

You should be looking to disqualify as many inappropriate and low-quality leads as possible with a self-service diagnosis which does not waste your time or theirs.

Conventional marketing thinking says keep your lead form as short as possible. Instead, you should be making it longer or replacing it with an education process, disqualification, and a self-service calendar booking for only the right prospects.

This appointment booking has a value, because it converts to the next step in the sales process, then the next, then the next, until finally you get paid. Each step has a conversion rate, and you must keep this process as short and as fast as possible to reduce abandonment and keep the money tracking simple.

Package your time

The key to selling your service online and making money is knowing it's value, date, time, duration, location, cost, if it's one-to-one delivery, or one-to-many or many-to-many, and using digital bookings to package it up, market it, make it self-service and where possible take a deposit or full payment online or be guaranteed a payment on a booking.

How much is your time worth? How much does it cost?

Your online business is going to struggle if you can't get paid within 30 days from an initial ad click and sales contact which you can track, or if you have so complicated a sales process you don't even understand it yourself, or have multiple departments who don't communicate with each other, or a fixed marketing budget you can't reinvest when you're actually making money.

The money questions

I asked my transfer client some pointed questions about his bookings, like "What's your no-show rate" (practically zero) and "Any cancellations?" (again, nearly zero). "What's your maximum target cost per booking (£5.00). "What's your average route price?" (£90.00). For ten years, this client has spent on average £4.16 per booking, making a *Return on Ad Spend* (ROAS) of 21.08 (that is 2,108% which means for every £1.00 in ad spend he makes £21.08).

Cost ?	Bookings ?	Booking cost ?	Booking rate ?	Booking revenue (£90.00 ave) ?	ROAS ?
£667,310.89	152,237.00	£4.36	15.52%	13,754,070.00	21.08

ROAS 21.08 - £21.08 revenue for every £1.00 in ad spend

Self service bookings

The online booking industry is exploding.

Think how many things you already take for granted as an online booking purchase, like a plane ticket or an airport transfer. There are hundreds of booking solutions for business-es, both general purpose and for extremely specific niches, like limo rides, salon or retreat management and many others.

Even *Google* is getting involved with their *Reserve with Google* program in the USA. If you don't get how important online bookings are going to be, you're completely missing the next wave of opportunity.

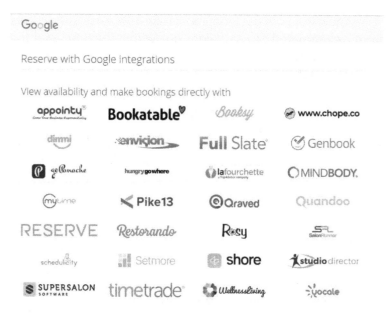

So, how are *you* going to get *Fully Booked* from online advertising?

Ads are answers

There's really only two kinds of advertising in the world (1) *Interruption* – think *Facebook*, TV, radio ads, web pages and those pesky ads which stalk you everywhere you go.

Then there's (2) *Search*.

According to *www.internetlivestats.com* there are over 65,000 *Google* searches every second.

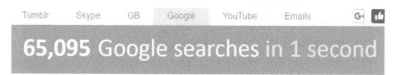

In this new age of GDPR, *Search* is the ultimate in permission-based marketing.

Why? Because people are looking for you. They want to find you. They *expect* to find you – right NOW. They will buy from *someone else* if they don't!

We know from our data that more than 30% of website visitors from well-targeted ad campaigns buy within the hour after the ad click. If you have the offer they're looking for, not showing up in *Search* results is not an option.

SEO? Too slow

SEO is a long game, and the common myth of SEO clicks being *free* is all wrong. If you haven't *tested* your offer and find that it sells with Google Ads, what's the point of SEO? You'll waste time and money on something no-one may even want to buy.

Hours to conversion ▼	Conversions	Conversion Value	Percentage of total ■ Conversions ■ Conversion Value
<1 hour	633	633.00	37.79% / 37.79%
1 hour	61	61.00	3.64% / 3.64%

37.79% of visitors buy within the hour

The stupid tax

The world is full of advertisers and agencies buying clicks from *Google* to sell products and services and make money, and many have no clue how to do it and are making all the same mistakes today they were back when it all started. Is that you?

The *stupid tax* means *Google* gets paid even when you don't, and because of it they are one of the wealthiest companies on the planet – on your dime.

Am I saying, "Don't buy clicks?"

No. Just the opposite.

You have to.

I'm saying you *need* to buy clicks.

But only when you know what they're worth. To YOUR unique business. Make Google pay YOU.

The Click Economy

Google sells clicks, but you sell services and products. *Google's* mission is to sell more clicks because this is what makes them the most money, and they have an inexhaustible supply of clicks.

But their problem is that most advertisers who buy clicks don't know how much money they are actually worth. Because if they did and they were profitable, they would buy more, not less.

Many advertisers limit their bids and budgets because they don't know if they're making any money. This is cost-center thinking. Or they have given up on *Google Ads* because they think it doesn't work. It does. What they really mean is they couldn't make it work for their business because they didn't understand how much the click was worth.

Budget ?	Status ?
US$255.00/day	
US$60.00/day	Limited by budget ?
US$10.00/day	Limited by budget ?
US$10.00/day	Limited by budget ?

Spending less not more - cost center thinking

Show me the money

The great Internet visionary and pioneer Ken McCarthy coined the term *traffic plus conversion equals profits*. And it's great wisdom, but not quite the full picture. Because you can buy clicks, convert them to leads and then even sell stuff as a result – but still go broke.

Perry Marshall perfected it with the *Tactical Triangle - traffic plus conversion plus economics*. But that's still back to front.

Because you have to know how much money you can make and how your sales process works and converts BEFORE you start buying clicks. Complicated sales processes can sometimes be simplified with just a small change in your workflow.

Systems Integration

Conversion and revenue tracking from *Google Ads* campaigns, correctly integrated into your sale process are the heart of making money with online advertising, but have to be setup correctly. And being cookie-based, will only work if the visitor doesn't block or clean cookies or change devices after the ad click.

Sales and revenue can be tracked this way for up to 90 days.

Get Fully Booked

So, in conclusion, to make money online and get *Fully Booked:*

1. Understand your *Average Order Value* and *Customer Lifetime Value.*
2. Get a detailed understanding of your sales process end-to-end and make sure it's as short as possible and every step is online where it can be tracked.
3. Calculate your capacity because selling services requires a calendar.
4. If you're not using a booking platform and relying on leads, try one out for free (say *BookingBug,* which supports *Google Ad* tracking built-in).
5. Take online payments only, even if a phone call is involved.
6. Track sales and revenue from campaigns so you know exactly how much money you're being paid.
7. If you're outsourcing any of this, make sure whoever manages it understands all these points.
8. If you can, find a strategic partner who only gets paid on results to minimize risk.
9. Get our *PPC Money Audit* of any existing campaigns to truly know whether you're making any money, or simply just giving it all away for nothing.
10. Get in touch to find out how much money you could be making if you were *Fully Booked!*

About David Rothwell

David Rothwell is the *Google Ads Money Expert* and has 13 years digital sales experience with *Google Ads, Google Merchant Center* and *Google Shopping.*

He is the author of *The AdWords Bible* for eCommerce and founder of the world's first *Google Ads £20k Challenge* – make up to £20k in 30 days, commission-only.

David's world-wide clients make money on a commission-only *share of the profits created* basis, not the typical agency model of a percentage of ad spend. This game-changing profit-center strategy means everyone wins, from customers, suppliers, payment processors to shipping companies.

David's attitude is completely different to other agencies. He counts transactions and money instead of simply counting clicks or leads. His unique engineering approach stems from over twenty years in the IT industry including *Olivetti* and *Hewlett-Packard,* and managing European IT, telecoms and support for *KLA-Tencor Corporation.*

David has been a certified *Google Partner* since 2005. He has spoken at conferences for *Perry Marshall, Ken McCarthy, PPC Hero* and *TeCOMM* in Maui, London, New York, Chicago and Bucharest.

He is referenced in Marshall P. (2014) *'Ultimate Guide to Google AdWords'* Entrepreneur Press, and Jacobson H. (2012) *'AdWords for Dummies'* John Wiley and Sons Inc.

LinkedIn: https://uk.linkedin.com/in/davidrothwelladwords
YouTube: https://www.youtube.com/channel/UCmMCXWUKLt-vC7sxT9fPRaEQ
Facebook Private Group: https://www.facebook.com/groups/MakeGoogleAdsPay/
Facebook: https://www.facebook.com/DavidNRothwell
Twitter: https://twitter.com/DavidRothwell
Website: http://davidrothwell.com/

"Fully Booked – How to Sell Your Service and Turn Time into Money": https://www.amazon.com/Fully-Booked-Sell-Service-Money-ebook/dp/B079814N21

"The AdWords Bible for eCommerce": https://www.amazon.com/AdWords-Bible-eCommerce-Counting-Clicks-ebook/dp/B00P714WTC

Amazon author bio: https://www.amazon.com/-/e/B00Q0297J2

The Difference That Makes The Difference

Angus Mac Lennan

In this hyper connected world where so many businesses are vying for people's attention and money, it is getting harder and harder to get noticed. Getting your message in front of your ideal customer is a challenge in the noisy online and offline world.

I get business owners asking me the same thing again and again – "How do we stand out?"

My answer to them, each and every time, is that they need to be *The Difference that makes the Difference*. To stand out they need to be different by being the best! Being the best is all about what I call the *Customer Journey* and *Customer Experience*.

Get it right and the magic happens, get it wrong and no one buys from you.

Most businesses are selling the same or similar products as other businesses so being unique is becoming more about branding and the experience the customer has when they deal with your business. Unless you want to compete on price alone and engage in a race to the bottom, you must look to what makes you better than the next business. Your product or service may feel unique to you but to your customer it is one of many they can find by spending five minutes searching online. You must offer the best experience in order to succeed.

Being the difference that makes the difference is about standing out, making a massive impact and turning your customers into raving fans who buy from you again and again. They will go on to sign up to your next level product or service and tell everyone they know just how great you are!

You can take the guess-work out of making your business successful by creating simple repeatable processes that make dealing with your business extra special.

Let me explain how you can create a special *Customer Journey* and *Customer Experience*.

The Customer Journey

People want great quality, good price, special service and a top notch experience. All that takes time and effort for a business to get right so many businesses only focus on getting part of the equation right. If you get the whole process right your business will stand out and become known as the best.

The full *Customer Journey* process is broken into the following section:

- Initial Awareness – where they first come across you
- Engagement – they engage with you in some way
- Connection – you take the opportunity to connect with them and start a conversation online or offline
- Meeting or call – you talk face to face or in a call
- Conversion – they buy into your product and business and make a purchase
- Upsell – you have identified what they need so you can genuinely and honestly sell additional products and services to ensure they get what they truly need.
- Service or product delivery – you deliver on the promise of your marketing and sales process and give them the best product and service and the best customer experience
- Raving Fan – by giving them service above and beyond what they expect and following up with amazing after sales service you are turning them into raving fans. This is where you then ask for referrals, reviews and testimonials. Make sure to have this as part of your process.

To create your customer journey, break down each stage in your business to its most basic parts and recreate it from the ground up with your customer's personal experience in mind (see below).

For example – every aspect of your meeting or call stage must be thought through and crafted. Do not leave any part of it to chance - so have your process written up and in place, pitch ready, answers to all the questions you get, develop an easy buying process.... the list goes on. Break down every single part of each stage and rebuild it with the experience in mind.

If you are a one person business then every aspect of this process is yours to design and implement. You must create every stage as if your business survival depends on it – because it does!

If you have a team then assign stages to team members and have them design and implement their part of the process. Let them own their stage but task one person to be in overall control of ensuring the whole process is crafted and delivered exactly as it should be to WOW your customer.

Every single step within each stage matters. Get it right and you have a repeatable system for growing a strong successful business with very happy customers.

The Customer Experience

The Customer Experience is designed with a single-minded intent - to deliver the best service and experience for the customer as they go through their journey with you.

To develop this part of the process you look at the full *Customer Journey* you have created and ask yourself the following at each stage:

- How easy is this for the customer?
- How will they feel?
- How does this look, feel, smell and sound to them?
- What do I want them to feel?
- How can I make it even better?
- What can I do extra that will make this over the top amazing?

- What process must I have in place to deliver on that?

You want them to feel like you are the only place they should buy from - so that even if they do not end up buying from you they will tell people how amazing the experience was.

How you make the customer feel is critical to your business success. In this busy internet age it makes all the difference.

Let me give you a couple of examples of where the Customer Experience has helped transform a business.

The Experience in Practice

Example 1

Niamh runs a wedding dress shop and the experience she has created is second to none across the whole county.

She has mapped out and implemented her full *Customer Journey* and has created a *Customer Experience* that has made her the difference that makes the difference.

Most of her requests for appointments now come from word of mouth both online and offline and from a personal and friendly social media marketing campaign that mixes high-end branding with a personal touch.

When her brides come to the shop they are met by a beautiful store front, young and fresh branding and two large cherry blossom trees. Inside is a scented store, an eight foot flower arch, flowers and accessories selected to deliver a WOW feeling. The bride and her squad are invited in and told that the shop is their exclusive changing room for two hours. Their space is a plush sofa with stools and a coffee table – all bought to match the branding.

They are then told how the relaxed and fun process works, offered Prosecco or non-alcoholic drinks and provided sweets and biscuits. A carefully selected playlist plays in the background as they get to 'play' with the dresses and select ones they like.

For two hours they are pampered and treated like princesses in their own private space. They are made to feel amazing!

It is so carefully crafted that I have only laid out a small part of the experience here. It is so detailed, even down to the scent sprayed before the bride enters – it seems there is a secret scent that is everyone's favourite.

The logic in creating this particular experience is that it makes the customer feel special – so special that if they do not find *The Dress* they still rave about the experience. It has helped take the shop from early stage to booked-up solid months in advance.

Niamh's process works so well because she understands each part of the Journey laid out above and has created a detailed and personal Customer Experience with the goal of standing out. It has worked spectacularly.

Example 2

This process works just as well for a service type business as it does for a physical products or bricks and mortar business.

My client Anna has used it to build a successful London based events company. London is a tough place to do business if you are an events company, especially if you are targeting the high -end corporate or high net worth clients.

The challenge for Anna was how do you get in front of the right people in the right way to give them what they need?

Anna has created a *Customer Journey* to help her get noticed, win business and create raving fans. Her marketing and sales process works so well because each stage has been created and implemented with the client in mind.

Within her Journey is an outstanding *Customer Experience* that is designed to ensure the person she is dealing with feels special and understood at every stage.

When her clients first come in contact with her she begins with a detailed discovery process that identifies what they need from the event. Once she has that clearly in mind she develops a briefing and proposal document, checks and holds the dates with all suitable venues and then submits the ideas to the client. This is hours of work done for free.

Her work gives the client a clear understanding of what is available, what can be done to create their perfect event and how much it will cost – all nice and simple with no hidden extras or obscure pricing. Transparency is key to her process as too many London clients have become jaded by the Events Industry which has a bit of a reputation for putting their own bottom line first.

Anna will attend the client meeting with all the standard slide decks and proposal but focuses primarily on relationship building. Her approach is to understand exactly what the client wants so she can deliver that – a simple concept but surprisingly not the norm for many in her industry.

Once the client is formally engaged she takes them to see the venues – covering all transport, drinks and meals so they just need to turn up and enjoy the experience.

As part of the ongoing experience, clients and their team are sent treats – Anna knows her audience well! They get pastries, cookies, sweets or if it is hot they get ice cream. She wants her clients to feel special because they are special.

All aspects of the event are handled from start to finish. No expense is spared on props, décor or staff and the focus is solely on delivering an amazing experience.

It is never about her bottom line – it is always about client experience. That is why Anna and her experience are the difference that make the difference.

Why Be The Difference?

In this crazy busy world you and your business must find a way to stand out and be noticed. We talk about marketing and social selling, we create customer avatars, develop our pitch and hone our skills. And then find ourselves up against other people doing the same things.

Keep doing all those things as they are important parts of the process.

But to truly stand out you must be different and that difference is to intentionally craft every single part of your *Customer Journey* and *Customer Experience* around delivering an amazing experience for your customer.

It doesn't matter what you sell. From widgets to high-end

services - build a process to turn your customers into raving fans and you will reap the rewards of happier customers and more sales.

About Angus Mac Lennan

Angus Mac Lennan is a Business Coach who uses a mix of real world business experience with targeted coaching, advice and guidance and Neuro Linguistic Programming (NLP) to help his clients achieve their goals and dreams. He weaves into his work a unique blend of Stoicisms and the African Humanist philosophy Ubuntu. He believes that 'we are who we are because of who we all are' and this is reflected in his businesses and his charity work.

His mission is to help people who have escaped the corporate grind to grow an ethical and fun lifestyle business that supports them and their team with the income and lifestyle they want, giving them the time to see and do the things they want.

He helps businesses to be the difference that makes the difference to their clients and the world around them.

Life is for living, not existing.

https://www.linkedin.com/in/angusmaclennan/
http://www.angusmaclennan.com

Storytelling For Sales Success

Robert J. Smith

Imagine that you walk into your office tomorrow morning to be congratulated by everyone on your team. "No big deal" you say.

"As good as all of you are, someone has to lead the office in sales."

"You didn't just lead the office" says a co-worker.

"Okay, so I led the state again." you reply, "That's nothing new."

Another co-worker exclaims, "You didn't just lead the state."

You wonder aloud, "The southeastern United States?"

A chorus of "No!" is the response you hear. "The United States?"

A resounding "No!"

Then it hits you.

You reached #1 in the world in sales for your company.

That's exactly what happened to me when I represented *Mutual of New York (MONY)*. This can happen to you as well.

All you have to do is figure out how to make it happen.

That's why you're reading *Sales Genius*.

My guess is that I am just like you. I always did well, just not well enough to suit me. *MONY* had close to 10,000 agents and brokers before being bought by *AXA*, one of the largest financial service companies in the world. I was always in the top 3,000. I was just never at the top.

That was until I found the single missing ingredient to sales success. That missing ingredient was storytelling.

Storytelling sells books. Storytelling sells movies. Storytelling sells financial services. Lucky for you, storytelling sells everything under the sun.

And yes, the Tommy James and *The Shondells* song, MONY MONY was written when he was in search of a hook for a tune that his group had the music written for. He walked out of his New York apartment building one day, looked up at the MONY sign that displayed the time and temperature and he knew he had what he was looking for. He had the hook that would sell his record. That hook was the one missing ingredient to his sales success.

While we may not think of the music business as a sales business, it certainly is.

What makes a hit song a #1 song? You guessed it. Sales.

Tommy James hit #1 in the UK with MONY MONY. How strong was Tommy's MONY MONY hook? Two decades later, Billy Idol covered MONY MONY and reached #1 in the United States with it as well. I've interviewed Mr. James for my upcoming book, #1 where we cover sales hooks in detail.

To reach the pinnacle of success in your sales career, you need a hook. You need the one missing ingredient.

You need storytelling.

It's likely that you have a scripted sales pitch that seldom varies. The reason that it seldom varies is that it works for you.

The question is, "Does it work well enough for you?"

If it doesn't, simply stick with that sales pitch until you create an opportunity to tell a story within it. Your first story may not work. Keep developing stories until you find one that works for you. When it does, incorporate that story into each and every sales pitch you make. Watch your sales soar when you do!

Here's the key for me. Tell factual stories. Tell stories that make sense to your prospects and clients. Here's how to do so in the most efficient way possible.

Determine the biggest obstacles to your sales success and eliminate them.

In four decades of financial service sales, I've found that there are two things that kill sales in that line of work. *Procrastination* and *Indecision*. It's likely that these two common obstacles are thwarting your sales success as well.

If you've ever heard the objection, "Come back and see me next week, next month or next year" and you've been unable to overcome it, then prospect and client procrastination is costing you sales and money. If you've ever heard the objection, "We want to think about it" and you've been unable to overcome it, prospect and client indecision is costing you sales and money as well.

I knockout both procrastination and indecision with my story about THE ADVENTURES OF INSURANCEMAN.

Actually, I don't even have to knock them out.

INSURANCEMAN literally knocks them out for me. This worked so well the first time that I tried it that I never looked back. Within a year of inserting storytelling into my financial advisory practice, I went from a top 3,000 ranking to a #1 ranking out of roughly 10,000 agents and brokers.

Storytelling worked so well for me that I created a print version of THE ADVENTURES OF INSURANCEMAN for licensing to insurance and investment advisors:

http://www.robertjsmith.com/

the-adventures-of-insuranceman/

These advisors have the ability to customize my INSURANCEMAN story into their practices and the companies they represent. I've also hired *DC* and *Marvel* artists to complete marketing and sales pieces for the mortgage industry with THE LOAN ARRANGER and the real estate industry with REAL ESTATE WOMAN.

Why do I pay some of the world's top professional comic book artists to illustrate my sales and marketing materials? One proven reason: A picture is worth a thousand words.

Actually, one of my pictures was worth $110,000.00 to me in a single day. I had recommended a large life insurance policy to an estate planning client.

When the only thing that stood between that six-figure commission and me was how he was going to pay the premium, I put a pencil in his hand and asked him to draw a picture of the dream house he was building for his wife and himself. Space limitations here prohibit me from telling that full story. The good news is that story and that picture may be found here: *https://www.robertjsmithproductions.com/online-store*

Never underestimate the importance of getting your prospect or client involved in helping you make a sale.

In the example above, just having my client draw a picture of his new home and getting him and his wife involved in my story wasn't quite enough to close the deal. I was at the goal-line, I still had to push the ball across it and into the end-zone for a touchdown. You should be able to guess what I did, and you should be able to use the same strategy in your sales business. That's right.

I asked my client to sign the masterpiece that he created.

The second he signed the picture that he drew, he took ownership of it. He also took immediate ownership of the life insurance policy that I recommended. Signing his picture also made it easier for him to sign his life insurance application.

It was a natural progression.

By the way, if you want to increase sales, it always makes more sense to sell larger priced items to prospects and clients whom you already have than it does to spend more money to attract more prospects and clients. By increasing sales to your existing prospect and client base you increase your revenue per prospect and client without increasing your cost of obtaining new prospects and clients.

My team and I have the ability to create stories that will help any salesperson close more business in any industry.

Our stories are created with a proven three-act structure that I created by blending what I learned by earning two screenwriting degrees simultaneously.

While the east coast philosophy that I learned at *Full Sail University* when I earned my Master of Fine Arts degree in Creative Writing as Valedictorian differed from the west coast philosophy that I learned at UCLA when I earned my *Feature Film Writing* degree *With Distinction,* I was able to blend the best of both philosophies.

I can use that advanced storytelling structure to create stories for you. However, if you want to create any kind of story, simply follow the three-act structure created by Aristotle.

Every story has a *beginning, a middle and an end.* This is what I teach in writing and public speaking classes.

Storytelling has proven itself to increase sales in every industry. The reason is simple. Storytelling is wired into our DNA.

We've been telling stories to each other since the beginning of time. Storytelling is how we relate to one another as human beings. What does the profession of sales amount to if not building relationships and connecting with prospects and clients? If you want to instantly increase sales, create stories that deal with and eliminate the objections that you most often face.

If you have trouble doing so, call us at +1 (407) 508-0200. We're here to help.

Storytelling will increase your production.

Storytelling will catapult your success.

How fast and how far you increase your production is entirely up to you. No matter what your sales goals are, we're here to help. Whether you want to improve your sales talk by adding a small story or you want to improve your sales by revamping all of your sales and marketing materials, the choice is yours.

Just start moving in the right direction and start moving in the right direction today.

About Robert J. Smith

After reaching #1 rankings and setting production and achievement records at *BankAtlantic/BB&T, Mutual of New York (MONY)/AXA Equitable, John Hancock and New York Life*, Robert sustained severe spinal cord injuries which ended his financial services career.

While undergoing fourteen surgeries and years of physical rehabilitation, Robert began training for a second career by concurrently earning his Master of Fine Arts in Creative Writing as Valedictorian at Full Sail University and his Feature Film Writing degree at UCLA with Distinction. Now, Robert is dedicated to teaching others how to overcome adversity and how to reach the top of their chosen professions.

Robert shares his proven storytelling methods, persuasive writing techniques and sales closing style with professionals through public speaking and private consulting to assure their success. In a career that spans four decades, Robert is the only financial advisor in the United States who has earned the CLU®, ChFC®, LIC, CCCC, RIA, AAMS®, CMP®, and CMPS® professional designations.

By creating THE ADVERTURES OF INSURANCEMAN, THE LOAN ARRANGER and REAL ESTATE WOMAN, Robert has provided financial professionals with the ability to lead their companies and their industries in sales production. Robert is available to guide salespeople to #1 rankings in all industries.

http://www.RobertJSmith.com
http://www.IMDb.Me/RobertJSmith
http://www.RobertJSmithProductions.com
https://pro.imdb.com/company/co0599398/?ref_=fn_al_co_1

Santa Is The Best Salesman On Social Media!

Steven Thompson

I want to share with you the best way to sell your products and services authentically.

But why do I have the audacity and outright nerve to say this is the best way?

It was the cornerstone for the setting up of my own business *BIGDaddyPR*, five years ago with zero invest and just a mobile phone.

The keys are a mobile phone, zero investment, my process and social media.

I want you to come on a short journey with me as to how I realised in sales you need to live like Father Christmas.

With today's technology, you will be able to 10X your results just like I did, turning my sales into 6 figures in my first full year of business.

One quick thing, before I start, I make no apologies for this story, I love telling it, I've seen so many peoples eyes light up and literally watched people have their aha moments before me.

I will give you my processes and a daily practice for you to put into action so you can win and live life on your own terms.

Tweet me *@MrSteThompson* as soon as you pick up my keyword _____.

In June 2013 I was made redundant from a job I was actually enjoying since leaving the police service as a detective after ten years.

In July 2013 my second daughter was due to be born, I had no job, a heavily pregnant partner and an ex-wife who my eldest daughter lived with and no way of paying maintenance, you can imagine where my head was at.

One afternoon I heard an advert on local radio, *Radio Norwich*, UK, the home of *Alan Partridge*, they were looking for business sales executives and that was something I knew I could do standing on my head, however, I didn't want to go back into sales.

When I left the Police I was forced back into sales with a *Vodafone Platinum* partner, doing B2B sales, because again needs must, however, I got straight out after having a heart attack through the stress I was hitting my targets but the company squeezed us sales guys for a stretch target, and so on. I was 34 years old.

But, heart attack or not, if I didn't get a job and support my family I would surely cause myself to have a second!

I contacted the radio station that afternoon, it was Wednesday, I was in their offices on Friday morning having an interview.

My interview was 0930, at 1030 I was out of the door and by 1130 I was home walking the dog when my mobile rang and I was offered the job. I was even given my first week off as my daughter was due on Monday.

Dreams and wishes do come true, or so I thought!

My daughter was a week late, so after my first day at my new sales job, my partner goes into labour, after an all-nighter my beautiful daughter Ruby arrives the following morning.

To cut to the chase though, I'm now into my new job as a sales guy, new daughter in my arms and the pressure is mounting that I need to put food on the table and pay the bills.

I literally had two days off with my family and was straight into sales mode, then disaster struck.

I actually found what I had to work with. The database of

clients and leads was awful, I quickly deduced that the two sales guys either side of me would rape and pillage the database of the cursed chair that I was sat in every 6 months when my predecessors left either through underperforming or unable to hack the stress of the job.

I needed a new way to bring in clients, I assessed what everyone else in the team was doing and saw a clear window of opportunity, I mean it was so big we could have plastered *Alan Partridges* face all over it and still have space for his name and novelty slogans.

What amazed me, even more, was the fact that no-one was doing what I was about to do, not even the radio station was making the most of their digital footprint.

So I jumped online, used my plethora of detective skills and brought myself up to speed on *Twitter* and *LinkedIn*, because let's face it, every business in this day and age was on *Twitter,* easily contactable and every decision maker had a *LinkedIn* account, can you see what I've done there already?

HACK 1 - HEAD START

Twitter is more likely than not, run by a marketing executive or the business owner, depending on the size of the business, the owner is on *LinkedIn* because that's where they think they should be.

We have just bypassed the Gate Keeper, no requirement for cold calling and out of date telesales.

HACK 2 - PERSONAL

I refreshed all of my profile and header images. I used my smiling face as my profile picture because people buy from people, not logos.

In my header images I added a picture of the inside of the radio station, for an added emotional hook I placed my then 11-year old smiling daughter in the radio DJ chair for added cuteness but more importantly relatability.

You guessed it, most people in business tend to have families, it was a soft touch but an emotional one.

HACK 3 - GIVE

I then proceeded to run through the poor database I had and see if these clients had a website and then find their *Twitter* accounts and simply retweeted their content if it was in date and relevant.

HACK 4 - DOCUMENT

With regards to what the radio station was doing, I simply told a story about my day behind the scenes at the radio station, build that anticipation.

Document over create, its a much easier and more socially acceptable, your content doesn't have to be polished and quite frankly you don't have time for all that. I certainly didn't I had a new job and targets to hit.

I'd started in August and through making people and local businesses feel special on social media I was soon invited in for a coffee.

I was making my profile look far more spectacular than the actual presenters and I was hitting my targets, my *Twitter* following was building up from a few hundred to a few thousand, people in the business community were beginning to know like and trust me.

I was giving them value online, my attention and I was being grateful for it.

Value - Attention - Gratitude = Legacy

In September we were given a product to sell to develop new business, it was called *The Local Hero Awards* imagine a local version of *The Pride of Britain* but on the radio.

We had 12 spots to sell in three weeks, what with all the normal pressures of targets and promotions to push out of the door, the sales team were stretched.

HACK 5 - HUSTLE

I literally hustled between 6pm and 2am on my mobile, *tweeting* and making connections, sharing the love to my prospects and building *Twitter Lists*.

Imagine it, last feed at 11pm, in a darkened room, baby in one arm and me trying to tweet prospects and get ahead all so I can hit targets and provide for my family.

HACK 6 - USE LISTS

I was adding all of my new leads and prospects into private lists on *Twitter*, then every morning I was going to my lists and wishing these people a good morning and *retweeting* their latest tweet or offer, this, in turn, gave them momentum and my audience began sharing their content, hence the coffee invites and the momentum of being known, liked and trusted, before they had even met me.

HACK 7 - CARE

Through the consistency of 'CARE'-ing for my new found online friends, doors were opened, coffee was had and sales were made.

Actually, due to the patience, caring and giving long before an ask was necessary it rarely felt like a typical sale!

It was actually an exchange of value!

I went into my sales meeting the following week and I kid you not, each sales guy had sold 1 awards package.

I sat there and had 4 sales in the bank and had four referrals to close that afternoon, which I did!

By 5pm I had 8 awards packages sold and the event went live.

My favourite memory to date about my new found passion for social media was when I stood drinking coffee on the shop floor of a reputable and classy 'love store' in Norwich.

Bunting and hay bales all around and the owner said to me,

"Steven I like you and I trust you, I love the idea of *Local Heros* but there isn't a category that fits our niche and clients"

We did joke about the *Good Neighbour* award but I could see his point, I suggested to him that if anyone could keep a relationship alive and fresh in this day and age of divorce and financial struggles that should be recognised and would he consider an award for *Romantic of the Year?*

HACK 8 - GIVE MORE

My suggestion was that I would replace an award that we hadn't sold with a bespoke award especially for him.

He laughed and didn't think I would get it past my boss.

I made the call there and then and pitched the idea to my boss, he went for it over the phone and the deal was done!

The most important thing that I had displayed through all of my sales processes and pitches to prospects and my bosses, was that I continued to GIVE and I CARED!

HACK 9 - CARE EVEN MORE

The most important thing in sales, no matter your process is to CARE.

CARE about your prospects and give them something they want, don't try to sell them what you have, GIVE them something that fits their needs and their requirements, this way they will be lifelong supporters of yours.

Yes you may well have a product or service to sell but if it doesn't fix their problem or provide a suitable solution to take their pain away then you're not serving them correctly. You might have won one sale but you won't win another because they will have your card marked and will see you coming.

Build trust, I did that by using social media, giving love through Twitter and sharing their content.

I then made a personal connection via *LinkedIn* and joined up their social media and gave them a *Facebook* like and shared their pages across other platforms for added value, tagging them in so they could see and introduced them to new connections, social networking.

As a result of this process and my success in caring I launched my agency in November and left my day job the following June, I've never looked back.

Social media doesn't have to be difficult, it just needs to be consistent and you need to be a practitioner, imagine if you did the following process for 15 minutes per day..

Where would your leads and meetings be at?

Think like Father Christmas. GIVE unconditionally and CARE.

1. Build private lists on *Twitter* - who do you want to connect with?
2. *Retweet* some of their content on a daily basis.
3. Start a conversation with them.
4. Connect with the company on *LinkedIn* and introduce yourself to the decision makers.
5. Continue to share and engage with their content across all of their platforms.
6. Provide links to content that would help them, with your thought and opinion.
7. Once rapport is built suggest a coffee or a meeting, by this point you will have had over 20 touch points and they will be liking, knowing and beginning to trust you!

Enjoy and Good Luck.

About Steven Thompson

Steven Thompson is the founder of social media agency *BIGDaddyPR* which he launched in 2013 with zero investment, a vision and a mobile phone.

Steven brings a unique set of transferable skills from 10 yrs as a police detective into his entrepreneurial life.

Steven truly believe's that everyone has what he call's a *Heart Brand* its the thing you would see and feel if you held that persons heart and soul in your hands.

It's the vision and deep routed values that will make our world a better place, where people of all ages, race and religion will be able to live the life they want.

Steven teaches people in schools, universities and businesses how to convey that message of purpose through storytelling via social media.

Steven's purpose and bigger vision is to improve the way young people are educated, and to teach entrepreneurs how to build a profile of purpose to achieve 'BIGDreams'!

LinkedIn
https://www.linkedin.com/in/steventhompson-socialmedia/
Twitter
https://twitter.com/MrSteThompson
BIGDaddyPR Facebook
https://www.facebook.com/BIGDaddyPRUK/
Steven Facebook
https://www.facebook.com/akaBIGDaddyPRUK/
Instagram
https://www.instagram.com/mrstethompson/
TEDx Talk
https://youtu.be/a6d41x1rUoo

Delivering Predictable Sales Performance

Marylou Tyler

Your ultimate weapon for scalably growing revenue lies in your ability to properly design and build agile, smart, processes for sales. Effective sales processes produce revenue streams for certain, dependable growth. Sloppy or nonexistent processes create tumultuous decay.

Assembling an effective sales process relies on structuring a few steps that, as a whole, consistently generate incremental revenue.

Those few steps form a purposeful system. A system of best practices that pave the way for sales leaders to implement, measure, iterate and improve on as markets or revenue initiatives and targets change or increase for the company.

The Painful Mistake Most Companies Make

One of the biggest misconceptions in creating predictable sales outcomes is to assume that adding salespeople and working them harder is what grows revenue. The old school strategy of hiring more *feet on the street* to drive revenue growth fails more often than not.

Working harder and *making more calls* doesn't scale.

Most salespeople already work enough hours, and trying to get them to work harder is like trying to solve a problem by going faster in the wrong direction. Bailing water out of a boat rather than fixing the leak.

Here is a scenario I personally see playing out for far too many companies:

- The board, CEO and leadership set an aggressive revenue target for the coming year (mostly based on new customer acquisition)
- The leadership (CRO, CEO, Sales) divides revenue targets by the expected quota of each salesperson to determine the number of salespeople needed to hit the target
- It takes much longer than expected to hire and onboard new salespeople, causing forecast to shift out multiple quarters
- Sales scrambles to pull future quarter projections into current quarter, missing targets, creating gaps, lowering prices to make book, leaving huge holes in the pipeline

Sound familiar?

Lead Generation Causes New Customer Acquisition

While it's true you need great salespeople to close customers, the better your lead generation is, the less dependent you are on the quality of those salespeople to prospect for new customer acquisition. Better lead generation = high confidence of hitting forecast month over month, quarter over quarter.

Let's do a quick comparison of these two companies. Which one do you think consistently hits goal?

Company A:

- **Goal:** Double from $10MM to $20MM revenue
- **Sales Staff:** 10 salespeople growing to 15 salespeople
- **Campaigns:** Generating $3MM new pipeline per month through proven campaigns focusing on
  - 40% Inbound (attracting prospects through multiple marketing channels);
  - 40% Targeted Outreach (Sales targets prospects with high revenue potential, high lifetime value, high likelihood of closing); and

- 20% Referral (current clients and partners refer prospects to Sales)
- **Sales Ramp:** 4 months. Salespeople walk into already-created opportunity pipeline from Inbound, Targeted Outreach and Referral campaigns

Company B:

- **Goal:** Double from $10MM to $20MM revenue
- **Sales Staff:** 10 salespeople growing to 20 salespeople
- **Campaigns:** None. But, VP of Sales and salespeople have a knack for hitting their numbers each month so far, with some scrambling.
  - Salespeople cold call;
  - Marketing dollars are spent, however there is no specificity of which lead sources generate revenue and what the mix (percentage of inbound, targeted outreach, referral) is
- **Sales Ramp:** Not sure - perhaps 3-6 months: No opportunity pipeline is created for the salespeople, thus ramp actually can take between 6-15 months, if at all.

5 Steps To Quantum Leaps in Performance in Sales

Here is an overview of a predictable process for effective lead generation - one that maximizes Return-On-Effort:

Step 1: Assess Your Market Potential

Get clear on what market segments you best serve, what your lead sources and mix are, and whether your universe of potential accounts fall into different buying scenarios.

Market segments typically come in two flavors:

- Market share (building or discovering new clients with new or existing products)
- Product share (intensifying or revitalizing existing clients with new or existing products)

Lead sources are the campaign channels designed to attract or target new clients. Typical lead sources are targeted outreach, inbound campaigns, executive briefings, referral sources, word-of-mouth campaigns, trade-shows, workshops, webinars, etc.

Lead mix consists of three types:

- Inbound (prospects engage with you through attraction-based channels)
- Targeted Outreach (you engage with targeted prospects who fit your ideal client profiles)
- Referral (prospects are referred to you by partners and/or existing clients)

Sometimes same product is sold differently.

Mapping accounts into different tiers of buying scenarios - cycles (lag), yield (conversion rates) and complexity (pipeline velocity) - improves forecast viability and allows for more focused sales conversations in lead generation campaigns.

Step 2: Target your best prospects

One of the biggest mistakes salespeople make is spending too much time with prospects who may never buy. Finding and selling to the right person to begin with is the most important renewal driver for a recurring revenue business.

The maxim *you can't be all things to all people* perfectly expresses the philosophy behind develop an ideal account profile. You do this by focusing on those companies or households with:

- High lifetime value (they remain your clients for a long period of time)
- High revenue potential (the initial sales revenue is high)
- High likelihood of closing (the yield [close rates] and cycle times [lag] are consistent and reliably forecast)

The process of efficient and effective conversations is enhanced by mapping out the roles of people we meet along the active pipeline - whether we're starting, or continuing conversation. *Ideal Prospect Personas* with influence maps (mapping out direct and indirect influencers who interact with the targeted persona) ensure salespeople spend their precious time focused on only those people who influence or advance the sale.

Step 3: Engage

Now that we've explored whom to contact, the next step is discovering how to engage those right people with the right sales conversation message.

Crafting the right message begins with recognizing that prospects exist at different stages of purchase intent in the customer buying cycle. Effective messaging paves the way for authenticity, starting with initial contact to explore joint values and proceeding through product implementation, delivery, and finally post-sale engagement and satisfaction.

For lead generation, we have additional considerations with respect to the use of technology in personalizing our sales message.

There are three degrees of personalization:

- Fully generic (lends itself to 100% automation)
- Mass-personalized (requires data to drive prospect-specific personalization)
- Hyper-personalized (human-assisted personalizing)

In the earlier stages of the buying cycle, mass-personalized communication will always be optimal. Regardless of strategy deployed, the level of personalization must increase during the later stages of the buying cycle.

Step 4: Measure, Analyze, Improve

Lead generation is not a set-it-and-forget-it process.

Salespeople must vigilantly measure and optimize their

pipeline to achieve maximum return on sales investment. A simple process you can deploy to improve your sales performance improvement involves five rules:

- Define what you want to improve or change
- Measure actual versus goal performance
- Analyze results by prioritizing issues and opportunities (impact vs. effort)
- Implement one new change and compare old versus new in a split test
- Establish a new baseline if new results beat old results

By adhering to these rules, you begin to establish critical metrics that serve as leading and lagging indicators of success at each stage of your pipeline.

Step 5: Systematize

Systemization involves arranging the sales pipeline into an organized, mechanized, high performing system that generates predictable outcomes.

The pipeline is filled with tasks that are performed over and over again. Some of these tasks lend themselves to technology, others do not. The more we can push to technology, while maintaining a high level of authenticity, the better. Because of your diligent attention to performance improvement, you've identified which tasks can be pushed more to automation versus those that require a high level of personalization.

Repeatable processes lead to consistent sales. And consistent pipelines improve your ability to scale.

Predictable Lead Generation
Leads To Predictable Revenue

Lead Generation is context-dependent in every imaginable way. Success depends on aligning the product (or service), the seller, and the prospect.

Although I cannot promise that lead generation is effortless,

I can promise that it is simple and straightforward. It can even be a little bit fun if you approach every day as a game by split-testing communication approaches, measure what works, and what doesn't.

At its core, lead generation is simply people selling to people. It's not about templates, scripts, or activities. Prospects need to connect with you and trust you as a partner who will help them achieve their goals.

If you stay organized and systematize what you can while maintaining your humanness, you will outperform everyone else.

About Marylou Tyler

Marylou Tyler is the Founder of *Strategic Pipeline,* a *Fortune 1000* sales process improvement consulting group.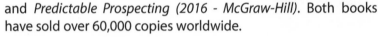

Her client roster includes prestigious companies - *Apple, Bose, AMA, Talend, CIBC, Gartner, Prudential, UPS, Logitech, Orkin, AAA* and *Mastercard.*

She is the author/contributor of two #1 Bestsellers: *Predictable Revenue (2011)* and *Predictable Prospecting (2016 - McGraw-Hill).* Both books have sold over 60,000 copies worldwide.

Marylou specialises in optimizing top-of-funnel sales process and implementing predictable new sales opportunity models. Her approach walks clients through a 7-point outreach process/framework that is part behavioral, part predictive and part creative (persuasive storytelling).

https://www.linkedin.com/in/maryloutyler/
http://www.strategicpipeline.com/

Can You Sell?

Andrew Priestley

Sales is the life blood of my business. If I don't sell, I don't eat. So I learned how to sell.

I coach professionals - CEOs, execs, owner managers. What I do isn't the cheapest and I don't try to be. It's a considered purchase. A high value, multi-step sale.

As my business grows I need more sales.

So I advertise for a salesperson. I field CVs, create a shortlist and then conduct some interviews. Everyone I meet *says* they can sell. And after several interviews, some careful deliberation and reference checking I hire a guy and put him in the field.

Almost immediately, he's telling me *no one's buying* despite the fact that I've built a sustainable six-figure business. He needs more product training. More time to get his feet under the desk. He wants 3-4 months to shine.

Ironically … he's selling me on why he can't sell coaching.

Another month goes by of *no sales* and now it's obvious …

He's a complete dud.

Now, I'm sitting here scratching my head wondering. He's a smart guy. Intelligent. His CV reads well. He interviewed well. His references were good.

And I'm a smart guy. *So, how did I miss this?*

I wish this was limited to just me but this is the story I hear from clients worldwide. Sales is the lifeblood of their business, too. And they are frustrated because they keeping churning through sales people … who *say* they can sell, but can't.

In 1991, I trained as a prestige real estate agent. The properties I was selling back then, were £2M+.

I did the real estate agents' course. A big component was the sales training and I top my class. Then I go out into the field and *none* of what I had blitzed in the classroom setting, worked in the real world.

If you've seen *Glengarry Glenross* or *Boiler Room* you will have an idea of the sales environment I trained in. And for a while I was the very bottom of the sales leader board.

My question was: *if I received world class training why wasn't it working?*

For the record I eventually ended up doing OK in prestige real estate but left to start an ad agency. The I decided to complete my psych degree where I learned about meta-analysis.

I started a meta-study of sales literature and courses and tracked selling principles right back to the early 1860s.

I identified over 256 sales factors but they cluster down to ten factors that follow the typical sales process for a high value, multi-step sale:

- Readiness
- Knowledge
- Prospecting
- Rapport
- Qualifying
- Presenting
- Closing
- Objection Handling
- Customer Service
- Administration

What I also discovered was those ten factors are moderated by three drivers: *attitude, drive to succeed in a frontline sales role* (called responsiveness) and *communication skills.*

In essence, you have two neat categories: *skill* and *will*. *Skill* is about *ability* and *will* is about motivation.

And I'm sure you know this already: often, someone with *high will/low skills* will out-perform someone with *high skills/low will*.

Part of my psych degree was designing psychometric indicators - scorecards or profiling tools. I took my learnings from the meta-analysis and created a tool called the *Sales Profile*.

Respondents answer 50 questions which generates a report that displays a graph of the 13 traits associated with sales ability. And it displays the two categories: *skill* and *will* so you can see exactly what's going on.

Uniquely, you also get detailed report with responses to how *you* answered key questions.

Importantly, the *Sales Profile* measures whether you can sell, or not.

Companies worldwide have been successfully using the *Sales Profile* since 2003 to make informed recruitment, management, training and supervision decisions about salespeople, because its easy to use and understand. It's in English, Russian and Spanish.

When I was researching sales profiles I discovered they were typically written by academics who've never done frontline sales. They were often so academic or complex, you lost the will to live trying to understand the recommendations. One profile I looked at made 84 recommendations!

The *Sales Profile* shows you what's happening but keeps it relatively simple.

You can see the 13 skills. You can see what's in range and what isn't. You can see the skills as they relate to a typical high value, multi-step sales process.

And it shows the drivers that moderate those key skills.

Subsequently, a sales manager can make clearer decisions regarding sales training or coaching, monitoring, supervision and support.

The Sales Skills Profile

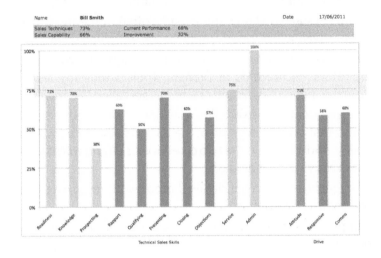

The Sales Profile. Chart 1. Name changed.

If you look at the chart above you can see a horizontal band around the 75% mark. If the vertical bars are *inside* that bandwidth, then that's a good game, keep it up. If the bars are *outside* the bandwidth - *high or low* - then it indicates sales training or coaching targets (usually validated by monitoring and supervision in the field).

Individually, each bar tells a story. If the bar is in range - nice game. If the bar is out of range on the high side you have that trait in excess. For example, a *closing* score out of range on the *high* side tends to indicate you are pushy. A *closing* score out of range on the *low* side indicates you might need to learn how to ask for the business.

The relationships *between* the bars also tell a story.

Bill (not his real name), is strong on *presenting* and *admin*, but low on *prospecting, qualifying, closing* or *handling objections.* Bill's *attitude* score is low - critical because *attitude* is the sales persons best friend - and he is low on *responsiveness* and *comm skills.*

If Bill had great technical knowledge I *might* hire but ensure he receives training and close monitoring and supervision.

I did some sales coaching with one of the UK's top engineering companies. Their engineers are analytical, highly technical *ask for the time and they build you a watch* people. So on this measure I expected to see high *presenting* scores.

Which is what happened.

By the way, on this instrument, we don't want 100%. High *out of range* scores on any trait usually indicates *over selling;* and low scores suggest *under selling.* Either end of the spectrum indicates you are most likely, *un-selling* prospects!

The engineers were responsible for sales but to a person their charts indicated high *presenting* scores. The risk here was they were drowning their prospects in a tsunami of information.

I dropped in to observe the sales training being offered by another supplier and the class were doing *closing* and *handling objections.* But they looked bored rigid.

I asked my host about the sales process. He said that under strict procurement laws they were not allowed to *close* prospects. They could *qualify* and *present,* but not *close.* That was done via an independent procurement process.

So why were they learning closing techniques?

I learned early that *skills* and *will* are great to know but only in relation to your *sales process.* See, you may not need to be proficient in *every* aspect of the sales process i.e., *closing.*

In this case, engineers were given warm leads. They needed to be great at *qualifying* and *presenting* only. But not *prospecting* or *closing* or *handling objections.*

I have worked with sales people who do lead gen through to the sale; and some who don't do any lead gen at all - just the actual sale.

The *Sales Profile* helps you measure skills relevant to *your* sales process. Useful.

In my experience of working with the *Sales Profile* since 2003, I have found that companies like it - especially sales managers - because its easy to understand. It's intuitive. They get the graph and love the detail in the report. They like the recommendations.

They like that it's been created by someone who has actually succeeded in a high value, multi-step frontline sales role. Someone who can sell.

And sales people like it because it gives them a very clear picture of what's working and what isn't. In my experience top salespeople always want to know.

There are two ways to access the *Sales Profile*. If you want to check out the online version go to

https://www.thesalesprofile.com

The online process is easy and fast and the PDF report comes back instantly.

If you'd prefer the old fashioned way via an *Excel* questionnaire, where you want to put *your* company details on the report, let me know. Likewise, if you need it in Spanish or Russian.

Contact me via *LinkedIn* or via my website.

I would say the number one reason to use the *Sales Profile* is it will save you an immense amount of time, money and help mitigate the frustration of hiring salespeople who can't sell.

Even if you don't use my indicator, profiling works, so look around. There's plenty out there. I'm not a fan of personality measures because personality is actually not predictive of the ability to sell. My accountant has the personality of a geranium but sells plenty. My profile has won several awards so you are in safe hands.

All of my clients need a sales engine that works. I discovered that a salesperson who can't sell will cost me a lot in time and money. Maybe you've discovered this, too. Profiling helps you get the right people and hire with eyes wide open.

Hope this helps.

About Andrew Priestley

Andrew Priestley is the managing director of *The Coaching Experience*, a multi-award winning business coach, ranked in the Top 100 UK Entrepreneur Mentors, a business strategy expert, an in-demand speaker, publisher, and #1 bestselling author.

He has always worked in big ticket, high value, multi-step sales environments.

Qualified in industrial and organisational psychology he is also the Chairman of *Clear Sky Children's Charity, UK* that provides much needed child therapy to children aged 4-12 who have witnessed or directly experienced a trauma.

He speaks on leadership, strategy, bizdev ... and sales ... worldwide.

www.andrewpriestley.com
Search Linkedin

https://www.clear-sky.org.uk

Would You Like To Share
Your Sales Genius?

Sales Genius is a #1 ranked and bestselling *Marketing and Sales* Amazon series written by high performing sales professionals.

We'd love authors for the next *Sales Genius* book.

Here's how it works.

Basically, we need around 1,500 words. Your story should be an original story that generously shares your sales expertise. We also need a short bio - 200 words about you - some links, a high res colour headshot (600kb+ JPEG) supplied as separate attachments.

There is a very small token fee to participate but collectively this splits the set-up costs and ongoing admin.

If you'd like to know more, email *coachbiz@hotmail.com* and we will send you the *Sales Genius Writers Guide.*

Lightning Source UK Ltd.
Milton Keynes UK
UKHW04f0627071018
330082UK00001B/258/P